"My Father's Daughter" offers many things, but perhaps most of all an honest view from the outside of the current American spiritual scene. Born and raised in Africa, the daughter of a famous African evangelist, Victoria describes in a very personal way her experience living in the United States. Her struggles have been both with the state of morality and spirituality in the U.S. in general, but also with America's Christians and churches. When Victoria gives her stirring call to revival, I can testify that it doesn't come from someone whose Christianity is lived out inside a church, or in a writer's study. I have had the privilege of seeing her every week on the streets and in the homes of the worst neighborhoods, with the addicts, with the drug dealers, with the felons both in and out of prison, with those struggling to hang on to a decent life, and with the saddest of all, those who have given up hope. Victoria isn't calling us to go into action, she's leading. I pray that many will hear Him calling us through her.

Michael Plesset
Operation We Care

My Father's Daughter

...Continuing the Dream for Peace and Reconciliation

Victoria Wilson Darrah

Published in Pasadena by
SERVANT WARRIORS PUBLISHING COMPANY
1997

My Father's Daughter

Scriptural quotations are from the New American Standard Bible, the New International Version, the Living Bible, and a healthy combination of the three.

For information write to:

Servant Warriors Publishing Company
P. O. Box 60047
Pasadena, California 91116-6047

Printed in the United States of America
First Servant Warriors Printing: November 1994
Second Servant Warriors Printing: February 1997

Publisher's Cataloging in Publication
(Prepared by Quality Books Inc.)

Darrah, Victoria Wilson
    My Father's Daughter :--Continuing the Dream / Victoria Wilson Darrah. -- 1st ed.
    p. cm.
    ISBN 0-9644039-0-0

    1. Darrah, Victoria Wilson. 2. Christian life--Biography. 3. Wilson, John E. H. 4. Anglican Communion--Uganda--Biography. I. Title.

BV4501.2.D37 1995   248.4
                                QBI95-20635

Front cover illustration by Albert Mukasa Wilson.
Back cover photograph by Cheryl Davis Sharp
Cover and book Design by Jim MacQuarrie

To John Wilson
May your light continue to shine
for many generations

And for Ken and Jordan
who bring so much love and joy into my life

A Tribute to Our Father...

My father's life
by Edward D. Wilson

Through my father's life, I came to see first hand what bliss can be experienced when one becomes intimately associated with deeply spiritual people who think in terms of the whole universe (the cosmos) as one incredible family where we can all live in peace, hope, love and dignity. People whose main motivation in life is GOD and COMPASSION. People who know the inherent worth and dignity of every human being, and the sacredness of Nature and Earth and all the creatures she contains.

Being in the company of my father was true bliss.

My father
by Albert Mukasa Wilson

My father was a big motivator in my life who was always supportive in my educational and career goals. He was a strict disciplinarian, and yet the most loving and caring father one would ever wish to have.

He was a very special man.

My father

by Philip Wilson

Above all else, my father was the person I turned to whenever all my efforts at solving a particular problem had failed. He had the never failing gift of reducing what would otherwise be insurmountable situations almost to insignificance.

Having his phone number in your pocket was like having your own exclusive AAA service. No matter where you were, no matter what the problem was, the solution was always at the end of that telephone line.

To me he was also the person who pinned the medal on my chest whenever I succeeded at something. No achievement was properly complete until I had secured my "Well Done".

My father was also the person I took with me when I wanted to impress a particularly difficult teacher or, as an adult, my employer. An introduction to my father dramatically improved my standing in society.

I am proud to have been his son, and feel genuinely sorry for those who never had the opportunity of meeting him.

Daddy

by Moses Wilson

Everything I know about being a man I learned from Daddy. Daddy was a son, a brother, a husband, a father, a grandfather, the voice of authority, the touch of compassion, a listener, a counsellor, a consoler and a friend. From him I learned to love my parents, cherish my brothers and sisters, treasure my wife, (and when the time comes, raise my children), to appreciate my friends and respect my acquaintances. From him I learned to analyze every situation, seek logical conclusions and implement appropriate actions. Daddy was both a great leader and a humble servant and from him I, too, learned to lead and to serve. Daddy taught me grace and poise and instilled in me confidence in myself. I am who I am because he was who he was - my "Daddy!"

Dad

by Daniel Wilson

Patience was a virtue possessed by a man who witnessed my rebellion against his dream for me, yet continued to shower me with unrestricted, unconditional love.

My biggest regret in life is that John Wilson did not live long enough to see the birth of the dream he had for me, the emergence of the responsible person he wanted me to be.

Daddy

by Elizabeth (Betty) Wilson

I remember those warm embraces every time he returned from his journeys. Somehow, he always kept his beard stubs for that moment and he'd rub them against my cheek...it made me laugh... Daddy's home!

My father was a house of strength, of power, and of wisdom. I admired how tirelessly he worked, the miles he traveled, the migraine headaches he suffered.... Even though we felt that he was overworked, he never complained. After all, it was all part of the job God sent him to do.

But after seeing the energy he put into God's work, I have always asked the question: "Why him, to die such a cruel death?" I guess we will never be able to understand why God does certain things in certain ways....

We LOVE you daddy! Always.

ACKNOWLEDGMENTS

My deepest gratitude goes to my husband, Ken; whose love, support and encouragement were invaluable in the writing of this book. He read each chapter as it 'rolled off the press' and his enthusiasm and insight inspired me to keep going. He has kept my life simple so I may write and be a wife and mother. Above all, his faith in me and in the call God has placed upon my life has given me the strength to dare to fly with eagles.

All the special people whom God has placed in my life deserve recognition for their contribution to this book, because they are a part of me, and I am a part of them. I owe much to my family, particularly my brother Albert whose artwork will always be a distinctive part of my work; and Daniel for being my sounding board and for dreaming the possibilities with me. Thanks to my sister-in-law, Grace, who also read each chapter as it was written and gave me spiritual encouragement and direction.

Special thanks to Michael Cassidy and the Right Reverend Bishop Misaeri Kauma, two very special heroes whose continued belief in me after my father's death has meant everything to me. To Connie Hinkle, thanks for being an eagle on the frontlines to save our children, and for being a special friend. How can I thank Jim MacQuarrie for all the pre-production work on the book? Jim's joy and enthusiasm have been a blessing. Many thanks, Jim for a terrific-looking book. Thanks to Mike Plesset for showing me faithfulness as we walk those streets, and for showing me how to study the Bible beyond the words.

Many, many thanks to Cheryl Davis Sharp, for capturing in pictures those last moments with my father: what an incredible gift. Jerry and Bunny Fish, the love you have for our family is beyond special. Thank you for the detailed final edit of the manuscript. Only the Lord gives such good gifts and we thank Him and praise Him for you.

Most of all, I would like to thank my son, Jordan. Your love for me is so wonderful. For the nights you stayed up to keep me company while I wrote this book. You have opened up my heart in a very special way and I love you with all my heart.

My Father's Daughter
...continuing the Dream

CONTENTS

FOREWORD

Truly, Victoria Wilson Darrah is her father's daughter. She is that biologically as well as in spirit as she seeks to fulfill her father's *dream*.

It has been our privilege and delight to know the John Wilson family. A number of family members have been guests in our home/s (in Kenya and the USA) and we in theirs. We were serving as missionaries in Kenya when we first came to know the Wilsons; we became friends while the family was in exile from their homeland, Uganda, during the reign of Idi Amin.

We two sat with Victoria's mother, Mary, in their home in Nairobi and wept and prayed with her after John's tragic death. We renewed friendship with Mary at the time we witnessed Victoria's marriage to Ken and heard them pronounce their vows to each other—vows which have lasted and will continue to last, vows which included the father's *dream*. Friendship with Mary was refreshed when we witnessed the marriage of Victoria's brother Albert to Grace. Albert—the brother who has done the art work for this production.

We became aware of John Wilson's *dream* when he was guest speaker at the Annual Missionary Retreat for the Kenya staff of World Gospel Mission in April 1977. He challenged us to be better Christians and better missionaries so we could help bring reconciliation to a fractured world—fractured from each other and fractured from God. We heard him emphasize his *dream* again as he spoke to a huge gathering at the large outdoor stadium in Nakuru, Kenya, on Sunday, January 22, 1978; this was organized under the auspices of the National Christian Council of Kenya.

Those who have heard Victoria in person will recognize her effective use of words in her writing just as in her speaking.

On several occasions we have listened to Victoria's witness as she spoke to youth groups as well as to adult audiences—she communicates and relates to all age groups. In our estimation she is fulfilling her father's *dream*. And she is doing this under the direction of the Holy Spirit and with His help. In MY FATHER'S DAUGHTER, Victoria bares her soul as she lets us in on God's dealings with her. She presents Jesus in a very personal way as He is there with her in her home and observes her as she battles through to victory at various levels of her spiritual walk.

May God grant that each person who reads this book will be challenged to "come out of the chicken pen" and "soar on eagle's wings" to help heal a badly fractured world.

Burnette C. (Bunny) Fish

Gerald W. (Jerry) Fish

Chapter 1

It's Time

My father, the Rev. John Wilson, was a man on a mission to reconcile people to God and to one another. It was a calling that had him preaching in places as varied as the grand cathedrals of Europe, to theological seminaries in Beijing. He preached from the pulpits of North America, to school rooms in Japan. He was as comfortable sharing his faith with Muslim sheiks in the Middle East as he was to business men in Africa. Although his was an international calling, he had a particular soft point for his beloved, but war torn country of Uganda. In 1985, after fifteen years of a seemingly unending cycle of death and suffering, my father sent out this challenge to the churches of Uganda:

> *"In a real sense the Ugandan crisis has its roots in moral decay. The people of Uganda have twisted minds. The change has to start from within each individual heart and mind. It has to start with a return to communion with God, then one to another. Churches in Uganda must come together to seek ways and means of reconstructing the hearts of the people of Uganda. We must join hands together and go out on our streets, and go out in our offices, in our hospitals, in our schools and entreat people to be reconciled to God. That is the first dimension that we must focus on, for how can we preach peace and reconciliation when the church itself is so divided? My greatest interest is to renew, revive and inspire the rising generation of Christian leaders to deeper, spiritual life and practical moral obedience. To stimulate, and to endeavour to meet the needs of the continent's emerging leaders, and to help them develop new skills and leader-*

ship qualities. To challenge and motivate them with imperatives of the great commission; proclaiming, winning souls, and discipleship."

Rev. John Wilson, 1985

By March of 1986 he was dead. Shot four times and left to die on a roadside four miles outside Kampala city. This was news I could not comprehend. I don't think a woman ever loved her father more. My love for him was complete and unconditional. His murder shocked the world of international evangelism. Telegrams from every corner of the world were sent to our family expressing the overwhelming sadness at the loss of this great man of God.

Shortly thereafter, in order to prevent my life from caving in, I delved into making a forty minute video documentary on his life and ministry as my tribute to him. Even in his death I needed to be connected with him, with his spirit. I wanted the world to know that a saint had lived among us, and I had been privileged and honoured to be his daughter. The documentary was a labour of love in cooperation with the evangelistic organization he had served as ambassador at large, and it consumed my every waking moment. A year later the whole project was brought to a crashing halt just prior to the final cut.

Over the course of that painful year I had developed a driving passion to preserve and advance my father's legacy. I believed that the visions the Lord had placed in his heart, and for which he had died, were the only paths to a future with hope. The shelving of the project into which I had shed so many tears was a major disappointment, particularly since the wounds were still so fresh. But being my father's daughter, and having studied and observed the best, I knew disappointments only made me stronger. Undoubtedly, there would be many more. I picked up his mantle and dedicated my life to the Lord to continue the fight for peace and reconciliation in his place.

Towards the end of 1987, I was twenty-nine and well into writing this book. However, over the following years it met with some rather stiff competition as the Lord turned my mourning into laughter. I married a man who was beautiful inside and out, and ten months later our beautiful son was born. I felt like I had climbed out of a deep, dark hole and was now proceeding up Mount Everest with new strength and vigour. The Lord had turned pure sorrow into pure joy. In whatever time I could repossess from my son, I tried my hand at different styles of writing: short stories, half-hour comedies, documentaries and screenplays. Then as my writing time increased, I decided to make another attempt to give my father the tribute I had not yet been able to give him. For two solid years I concentrated on writing and rewriting a screenplay entitled *Blessed Are The Peacemakers* - the story of a young African woman's struggle to go on after her father's death.

Nineteen ninety-three found me preparing for the eighth rewrite, but I was burnt out. I felt restricted in the film format. I didn't want to invent action and violence in order to tell my story, and what I wanted to say could not fit in little 3" X 1" spaces centered in the middle of the page. I prayed earnestly for direction and inspiration from the Lord.

One morning I woke up with a strong conviction that it was time to write the book. My first reaction was, "Oh, no! Not the film too?" Again I had to place on the altar a project into which I had poured my hopes and dreams. God was asking me to just trust and obey Him. He knew what He was doing, and He was still very much in control. Thankfully, this time I was picking up a vision I had placed on the altar a few years back. I was armed with a portable file cabinet containing color-coded folders of the twelve chapters of a book addressed to young African women.

Inside the folders, the chapters were at varying stages of life— from completed chapters to rough outlines. I read through the twelve headings and was greatly relieved to find I still believed in the topics I had chosen to write about. However, I was now thirty-five, a wife and a mother. My opinions had undergone many radical overhauls. Some I had thrown out, others I had refined; I was developing new ones and freeing others. My focus had become more global. I now saw a great need for a world-wide revival.

Six months later I held a two hundred and fifteen page first draft of *Call to War* in my hands. I sent out four proposals and to my delight the manuscript was favourably received, but again, I felt the Lord asking me to put the book back onto the altar until it was His time for it. I had by now accepted the fact that in God's personal school of leadership training, one simply had to go on faith. There were no guarantees, just surprises at every turn. Every prayer was answered as only God could answer it, and it was now time for the fulfillment of a long-standing prayer. In a miraculous and amazing move, He took me out of the church I had attended for eight years (very unhappily for the last three), and called me to lead another congregation as their interim speaker. For thirteen challenging weeks I stood behind the pulpit every Sunday morning and delivered to the people a message from God. I fell in love with them and they fell in love with me. I had found the church home I had been praying for so desperately, and it had been worth putting everything on hold for.

Now, as I sit at the computer again, contemplating the task of rewriting the book for the final time, I feel loved and supported. I feel like I can now create positively with words that bring healing. I am also re-inspired with new and wonderful information I would never have gained had I remained in my comfort zone. I now have a deeper understanding of the problems facing the world as we roll unsteadily towards the twenty-first century. I also have a new appreciation of the authority and Lordship of Jesus Christ. I have experienced the thrill of spiritual adventure, and have felt God's power beneath my wings. I have fallen in love with Jesus completely and without compromise, and vow to advance His name into all nations by whatever means necessary, and at whatever cost. I still dare to dream that revival is possible in this land.

I am an African woman. My mission field, for the present, is North America. I am commanded to be a light to the nations, to open blind eyes, and to bring the prisoners from the dungeon. My assessment of the situation: Americans are in the grips of the devil. They have allowed him too much access into their lives. They have made a deal with him, and are selling their souls for the temporal, the material. The forces of evil roam freely across the land, capturing and enslaving men, women and children, using the simplest of baubles to excite their imaginations and captivate their base desires.

While the citizenry continues to be preoccupied with the petty accidents and happenings of their lives, the political powers that be are changing the laws of the land in drastic ways and at fantastic speeds. Only the eternal optimist can still dream of creative ways to reharmonize this country. A large number of Americans, overwhelmed by the rapid decline of their society and feeling small and powerless to fight the government, have simply chosen to live in a stupor, making this the nation with the biggest appetite for drugs in the world.

Christianity, particularly in the Western world has lost so much ground it's hard to believe we can recover. I admit that I, too, sometimes despair. The Christians have decided to sleep it out, and so committed are they to their fruitless agenda that they get downright angry with those who try to open their eyes and get them ready for war. The Church in America has been asleep so long, we now have churches filled with men and women with no understanding of spiritual truth. People who are called by His name, sealed by His Holy Spirit, but refuse to humble themselves and seek first the Kingdom. People who attend church regularly yet refuse to renew their minds with the Word of God, and refuse to allow their hearts to be transformed by the miracle of salvation. They choose instead to cast their pearls before swine, panhandling for dimes in an increasingly hostile world. They have become spiritual paupers —the future homeless of heaven.

We have lost our visions and are perishing. We have sold our birthright. We no longer experience the privileges and joy of being sons and daughters of the living God. We have lost the respect and awe-inspiring mysteriousness that characterizes people of God, choosing instead to live lives of quiet desperation. Unfulfilled. Never quite learning how to soar in the Spirit. Never daring to taste the thrill of adventure.

Meanwhile, in the world around us, the quiet is not so quiet anymore. America of the 1990s is walking steadily towards civil war. More and more police officers are being trained and sent out into the streets to fight crime. Illegal weapons are entering the country at the tune of a million a day. On any given day, more than two hundred thousand children carry guns to school. Time magazine now has headlines like "America The Violent." Emergency rooms around the nation are overwhelmed by the shooting victims being brought in round the clock. The war against life has intensified. Laws that kill millions of unborn babies a year are continually being strengthened. Others are being passed to kill the elderly. Doctors are seeking the legal right to kill their patients.

Perhaps closer to my heart than any other group in the country is the upcoming generation of young people who are very appropriately called "The Lost Generation." An entire segment of society who have never been loved, who have grown up without nurturing or discipline and are engulfed by an emptiness that is fatal. Each day leads them closer to the edge as they get more hopeless, more calloused and more violent. Meanwhile, God's people sit on the Truth that can bring these young boys and girls into the wonderful knowledge of God's love. The Truth which brings good news to the afflicted, binds up the brokenhearted, heals the sick, and proclaims freedom to prisoners.

"BLOW a trumpet in Zion, and sound an alarm on My holy mountain! Let all the inhabitants of the land tremble, for the day of the LORD is coming, surely it is near." Joel 2:1.

This is a wake-up call. The Lord has sent me to wake you up. I am an alarm clock with no snooze button, coffee— no cream. We can no longer afford wimpy Christianity. It's time for an in-your-face Christianity. Like the prodigal son, we must 'come to our senses' and return once again to our only source of hope, Jesus Christ. It is time for a living faith that engages the mind. It is time for fire-proof faith, a faith matured in the experiences of life and personal testimony rather than a faith that is cowering in POW camps. If the Church of Jesus Christ is to make a difference in the twenty-first century, then we need a force of Christian soldiers that is tough and hard to bluff.

I write this book not as a sociologist, or a politician, or even a theologian. This is simply my testimony shared with those who are caught up in the struggle of life, seeking to find their purpose, preparing to flex their wings in the world, seeking to build rather than be a part of the forces that are destroying our beautiful world. My hope is to awaken the sleeping giant within us all. It is time to get out of our spiritual ghettos and become concerned about our political, social and economic climate, because those in charge have shown us consistently in the past that they don't share our values and beliefs. There is a great need for an authentic nation-wide revival. A spiritual awakening that will shake the very foundations of this country, destroying all the strongholds of evil and setting God firmly back at the helm of society.

I hope we can discover the steps we must take as individuals to turn around this tide of moral depravation that has gripped our hearts. These steps will not be simple, because there are never simple answers to complex issues, but they will not be impossible either. They will just require our collective commitment to change. We must first believe that God has a plan for this country, a plan for a future with hope, and that He is quite capable of making it happen. There are many parts of the world already experiencing major improvements in their societies in the name of Jesus. What about America? Can we not give Jesus a try? We certainly cannot afford any other choice, especially not the selfishness and indifference so prevalent in the Christian heart today.

If I can provide a little consciousness, shed a little light in your path of progress, then maybe you will 'light your candle' and help others along the way. We are in this together. Each one of us has been gifted wonderfully and uniquely, but all have been commissioned to the same purpose— to build the Kingdom and destroy all the works of the devil, starting in our individual hearts. We are accountable to each other and ultimately to God.

At the core of the ministry of peace and reconciliation that I inherited is the fact that in the Kingdom of God we are all brothers and sisters. We are to be brothers and sisters to one another. Until that fact hits us at the very core of our psyche, there will be no revival. God wants a united Church, nothing less. He is not amused by all the coldness we display to each other, especially in our churches—our places of "fellowship." Unless we shatter the prejudices that surround our souls we shall continue to bear the fruit of our disunity; selfishness, greed: and hatred born out of ignorance and fear. The devil will increase his strangle-hold on us. We shall continue to despair about the future, and the lost generation will grow in number and continue to be lost.

The ultimate responsibility of turning the future around rests heavily on the shoulders of the present generation of Christians, both young and old. It is imperative that we return to the basics of life: a heart that is pure, a love that is blind. We cannot, as much as we'd like to sometimes, divorce ourselves from our past, but we can determine not to be bound by it. We must choose instead to celebrate our individual uniqueness. We must recognize our joint power to create the humanity, the dignity, and the joyfulness of each one of us. We must strive together to ensure that no one ever has to live at a standard of life that is inadequate for the full development of his/her personality.

It is time again to train up leaders of character and strong moral backbone. Men and women, both young and old, who will dare to dream dreams and see visions. Servant-hearted men and women who will lead movements that will sweep the entire length and breadth of humanity, spreading the love of God in a practical, compassionate, very real and relevant way. It is time to embrace reality with a combination of grace and truth. It is time to "work out our salvation with fear and trembling."

"But an hour is coming, and now is, when the true worshipers shall worship the Father in spirit and truth; for such people the Father seeks to be His worshipers." John 4:23

It is now time for the true worshipers to give up fruitless lives of duty and boredom and experience again the joy of dynamic, God-inspired progress. It is time for the chosen generation to stand up and be a light to every nation. It is time for war. Onward Christian soldiers.

Victoria Wilson Darrah
September, 1994

Chapter 2

Thanks, Dad...

Perhaps no other woman in the world is as greatly indebted to her father as I am. He is the inspiration for this book, and I dedicate this chapter to all fathers and the daughters who love them. I recognize the great gift God gave me in my father, and how I wish every little girl, every young lady, every woman in the world would experience such a relationship with their fathers. How I wish every man who has a daughter would realize how important it is that they put on, and leave on, the light for them.

The contribution of women to the world goes far beyond their reproductive abilities. They make or break our societies, thus the well-proven adages like "teach a woman, train a nation," or "a country is only as strong as the character of its women." If our societies are failing, then we must take a closer look at the relationship between fathers and their daughters.

Recently, a well-respected pastor in Southern California made a statement on the radio. He said that the second most important relationship in a family structure, next to the husband/wife relationship, is the father/daughter relationship. A study done at Radcliffe, one of America's premier institutions for women, showed that the women who went on to excel in life were those who had received consistent, positive encouragement and input from their fathers. I can safely assume that the number of prostitutes with poor or negative father figures far outweighs those with good, positive father figures.

I have many female role models in my life; most of them are daughters of great fathers. The two most notable just happen to be politicians, but what fascinates me most about these women is what I share(d) with them— our relationships to our fathers, and our passion to continue their dreams. Benazir Bhutto, Prime Minister of Pakistan, and her much loved father, former Prime Minister Zulfikar Ali Bhutto. The late Indira Gandhi, one of the first women heads of state in modern history, and her father the great Jawaharlal Nehru of India. Another favourite of mine is Margaret Thatcher, former Prime Minister of England. Although she chose a different profession, a very special relationship with her father greatly shaped the Iron Lady.

When my father died in 1986, it was in the stories of Indira Gandhi and Benazir Bhutto that I found women who understood the loss of such a father. Sometimes God gives a man a child who is his soul-mate, who understands and shares his excitement and his dreams. In each of our individual stories this resulted in a mentor/student relationship with our fathers that was rooted in a tremendous depth of love, mutual respect and pride. Our fathers realized that if we were to become the women they wanted us to be they would have to teach us themselves. They went to tremendous lengths to include us in their itineraries, and didn't seem to mind little twelve year old girls traveling beside them and sitting in on their high powered meetings.

With their deaths, the era of playing supporting roles in their visions came to a close. We had to face the challenge of life ahead without them. Yet each of these servant-men had dreams so noble they could not be allowed to die. In the loving and training of their daughters, these fathers insured against it. Even though the task ahead looked formidable and we felt so alone, we knew that our fathers had taught us lessons that no man could take away. They would help us face what lay ahead.

In continuing our fathers' dreams, we insured that we would always feel their presence and influence in our lives. In my case, because of the wonderful gift that we shared of the Holy Spirit, my father would continue to teach me about the things of God as the Spirit brought to my remembrance the Jesus I had seen and admired in him. I wanted to be just like him.

My story began early one December morning when the doctor told my parents, already parents of three sons, that they finally had a little girl. They were overjoyed. They named me Victoria. My mother was relieved because she could now close up shop, or so she thought. (The Lord surprised her with two more boys and a girl.) Immediately there was a very special bond between father and daughter. Daddy and his little girl. He adored me and I adored him back. To see one was to see the other.

One of my early memories is of the family sitting at the dining room table. I was about four years old. Everyone had their special place at the table, and I had mine, on my father's lap. He and I shared a plate until I got too big for his lap; then I sat in a chair next to him. By the time the fifth boy was born, I was a confirmed tomboy, short hair and all. My mother, the best seamstress in town, was dismayed when I traded in her beautiful, frilly creations for tennis shoes and hand-me-down jeans, but I had to keep up with my father's long strides. I didn't invite my father to tea with little tea pots and cups; instead he and the boys welcomed me into their world of soccer and tennis.

He took me hunting and showed me how to track and shoot pheasant. At ten, I flew in an airplane for the first time when he took me with him on a business trip to Nairobi, Kenya. He handed me trophies at tennis championships, and clapped the loudest at my piano recitals. To him there was nowhere I couldn't go, nothing I couldn't do. With his example, I learned how to dream big. He opened the world up to me and I flexed my wings under his careful guidance. He set standards, and I shot for them with everything in me. He was the most important person in my universe, and I wanted him to be proud of me.

Above all, I never wanted that warm smile to fade off his face. I remember vividly the day he came home after a company soccer match. He had two very bloody knees. As my mother carefully cleaned and bandaged them his face winced in great pain. I remember hiding my face in his chest so he wouldn't see **my** tears. I hugged him tightly, wishing I could make the pain go away.

The true test of any relationship is whether you are willing to die for your friend. John 15:13, "Greater love has no one than this, that one lay down his life for his friends." There was absolutely no doubt in my mind that my father would have died for his family. It wouldn't be too far from the truth to say that he burnt incense at the family altar. No matter how much he traveled the globe fighting for peace and reconciliation, his devotion was always first to his wife and children. On his travels he kept in close contact through letters and the telephone. In 1981, I proved to my father that I would die for him.

I grew up in an exciting Africa. The early sixties saw the continent march hopefully into independence. In October 1962, astride on my father's shoulders, I watched the Union Jack being lowered and the Ugandan flag raised in its place, blowing proudly in the new winds of freedom. By 1981 Uganda had gone through the terror of Idi Amin and was now caught up in a post-Amin power struggle.

After graduation from USC, I had returned to Africa to be with my family who were living in exile in neighbouring Kenya. While my father and mother were away on a speaking tour in Europe, we received news from Uganda that my grandfather, my father's father, was very ill and needed to be brought to Nairobi for treatment. With my father out of the country, the only person that could go was my brother, but that would have been suicide. Young men between the ages of fifteen and twenty-five were systematically being captured and tortured, many even murdered. It was too risky.

I decided to go. Everyone thought I was crazy, but I was determined. My father's anxious voice on the phone haunted me. I wanted to go in quickly and bring his beloved father back for treatment. I began to work on getting a Kenyan visa for my grandfather. I sat in the visa office all day long. When my father learned of my plans, he cancelled the remainder of his tour and came home. I'll never forget the tears in his eyes as he hugged me so tightly I could barely breathe. My mother told me later that he had been greatly touched that I had been willing to risk my life to bring my grandfather back. The idea that I was risking my life had not been the issue, only my father's happiness. I knew how very much he loved his father.

A day later I was still determined to make the trip into Uganda because I would not let my father go in alone. I would rather they killed us both. We went in and returned safely with my grandfather, although not without some major and minor incidents along the way. I'd never been more appreciative of the clerical collar and the respect even drunk army men with guns had for it. They knew not to mess with a man of God.

There is no light brighter than the one that is lit from within. A father's primary function on this earth is to be a reflection of our heavenly Father. He is to love and nurture his family. He must be there for them, to provide for them, to protect them, to guide them in the ways of righteousness. By being a reflection of God to his children, a man gives his children the greatest gift of all, a love for God that is natural, exciting and revolutionary. He lights a beautiful fire within each child. A light that never burns out. A light that keeps on shining even after he's gone and the world around seems dark and bleak. A light that gives them the courage to stand alone even as the world around them rewards immorality and selfish ambitions. A light so many children in America are living without.

A sad fact in America today is that only one out of every ten marriages is truly happy. Five end up in divorce, the other forty percent range from miserable co-existence to just getting along. I am very blessed to be able to say my marriage places high in the ten percent that are truly happy, and I will always credit it to our parents, particularly our fathers who loved our mothers. The second greatest gift a man can give to his children, particularly his daughters, is to love and value their mother. My father often said the first thing he was going to ask God when he got to heaven was how He had allowed a woman like my mother to marry him.

I will always remember fondly, my father pulling my mother to him and hugging her. I remember his cards to her addressed to his dearest 'S as S'— Soft as Silk. I loved the way he always talked about his Mary. How he always went to tremendous pains to find something extra special for her whenever he traveled abroad. He knew her likes and dislikes, her dress and shoe sizes, even her favourite brand of stockings— size and colour. We always looked forward to my mother's birthday, because as far as my father was concerned it was a national holiday and we celebrated it in style at the poshest restaurant in town.

I saw how tall and proud my mother walked among the other women, like a queen, for she truly was his queen. With his full strength and support behind her, she strove for and accomplished her goals. I knew growing up that that was the way I wanted to be treated. I would never settle for a man who was less committed, or less caring. My father had set the standard. It was such an excellent standard that by my late twenties I had resigned myself to the single life, quite sure that such a man did not exist. Like Barbra Streisand's Yentl, I asked the question, "Oh, tell me where... where is the someone who will want to share my every sweet-imagined possibility?"

It is a fortunate fact for women with good father figures that we tend to marry men like our fathers. My father died before meeting Ken, but I knew he was the man God had chosen for me when my mother said to me, "He's a good man, just like your father." I had the strength to wait for God's perfect mate because my father had given me a voice, he had given me a choice. In loving my mother he instilled in me a sense of great value.

The next greatest gift a man gives his children is that of training them in the way in which they should go. I tell people my mother demanded perfection, and my father demanded excellence. Both qualities required great discipline. Being wise and compassionate, my father realized that rewards were a great incentive for achievement, so the higher the stakes, the greater the prize. He and my mother opened every door they could to expose my siblings and me to all the possibilities. My father was committed to giving each one of us the best education he could afford. He and my mother introduced us to classical music, and to our own heritage, and through his travels my father developed in us an appreciation of the many cultures of the world.

He also demanded excellence in our choice of friends. One day, while on a short stop in California, my father met some of my friends from the university. Later on he asked me, "But Victoria, don't you have any friends of substance?" My friends were a reflection of who I was, and he wanted me to be a woman of substance.

I remember him asking me one day, "So, you want God's best man?"

"Of course," I replied.

He looked unflinchingly at me and asked, "And what makes you think God just gives away his best men like that?" In order to get God's man, I had to be God's woman. In order to receive excellence, I had to give excellence.

My deep love for God is a direct result of how very deeply I loved and respected my father. In these tough times when people's understanding of God is muddled by the less than heroic quality of men today, the world is crying out for strong men. When acclaimed plays project the theme that it is natural to hate your parents, and that you will grow up and have children of your own who will hate you, then I think it's time for me to stand up and with a resounding "NO," put an end to such a lie. There are people who adore their parents and are raising children of their own who love them. To hate your parents is not natural; it is a sign of emotional sickness caused either by bad parenting, or selfishness. Even in rebellion, children with good parents do not hate them; instead they have major regrets over hurting them.

My natural love for my father was the spark that set the fire of the love of God within my heart. Christian men, this is a call to war. Declare war on wimpy Christianity. Put to death wimpy fathering. If your daughters are in dysfunctional relationships with men, and with God, it is time for you to determine to show true love and godly leadership. Your daughters need you to model your love for God, your love for the woman in your life, and your love and commitment to your children. Educate their hearts and minds to true greatness and beauty. Give them convictions to live by and die for.

I am ready to die for God just as my father did on March 16th, 1986. There isn't a day that passes when I don't miss him, when I don't feel a need to discuss the issues of life with him. My wound has for the most part healed, but there are times that a song, a picture, a memory, a certain smell will tear at the scar and it will bleed. Not for very long anymore, but just as brightly and just as deep. I am most grateful that I always told him how special he was and how privileged I was to be his daughter. This leaves me with no regrets. I feel sad that he never met my husband, nor got to see his grandson, but his light continues to shine brightly in my heart and I am passing it on.

Thanks, Dad, for giving me that most wonderful of all gifts, a very real and practical understanding of my ever loving, ever merciful, heavenly Father. Thanks for showing and teaching me how to live the Christian life. Thanks for the time, the thoughts, the prayers you invested in my life. When I get to heaven, my first objective is to thank God for allowing me to be your daughter.

I can now say just as you used to say, "I dream big dreams because I serve a big God." I pray that your example is a challenge to other men, for what the world needs now is more men like you. May the blood you shed for your God and your country be the seed of the church.

I can't thank you enough, Dad...for leaving the light on. May I be worthy of it.

Chapter 3

Shattered Crystal

Gayaza High School. It's six o'clock on a beautiful Ugandan morning. Young girls have been hauling heavy suitcases from their dormitories to the gate since five o'clock. It's one of three very special days of the year— when school lets out for the holidays. The spirit of excitement that has gripped the school for the past week is finally coming to its finale. Before nine o'clock most of the girls will be gone, picked up by family members coaxed up at ridiculous hours to make the one hour drive to the school. This is, after all, Uganda's premier boarding school for girls. Those who get picked up first win.

As the sun begins to creep onto the horizon, much of the luggage is safely lined up by the gate and the girls are in their dorms anxiously awaiting their dorm mothers' inspection. Many are taking this time to do some last minute primping. We must look good, not only for our parents, but to whomever we might see at the gate. Miss Cutler rounds the corner of my dorm just as I throw the tell-tale remnants of our midnight party (prohibited, universally practiced, last-night-of-school dorm parties) in the garbage can.

"Wilson! Ready to go home?"

"Yes, Miss Cutler," I mumble, as I slide past her into my room. She steps in with her sharp eyes and starts to look around. I hold my breath. My handsome, very popular brothers are coming to pick me up early and I want all the girls to see them. I can't risk any delays. Miss Cutler, a physical education teacher from England, is my favourite teacher, and I suspect she has a soft spot for me, too, in spite of the curt good-bye she bids me. She's going to let me play a couple of games with Arthur Ashe when he visits next term. Before I make a mad dash for the gate, I assure her I'm going to play every chance I get. She breaks out into a proud smile. I smile back, determined to keep my word.

I pass a couple of sleepy heads struggling with their suitcases. The early birds and their belongings already line both sides of the road for about a hundred yards from the gate, watching each car that drives up and parks on the other side. Those with recognizable family members are hailed immediately. With our adrenaline running on high, we exchange phone numbers with those who run in our social circles. I make sure those with brothers of special interest to me have my number. We discuss upcoming events— parties, weddings, church. We snicker at those whose parents come in taxis or in some way don't measure up, spoilt brats that we are. Daughters of privilege.

Shrieks and squeals erupt from those closest to the gate. My suspicions are confirmed when I see my three older brothers walking, no, strutting towards the gate. This is their moment and I am delighted to give it to them. I wait until they sign in at the gate before I walk towards them. We exchange brief greetings before I lead them to my bags. We joke about the way the three months have changed us. A close glance at Philip's face shows me where he has assisted his moustache. I crack up, much to his consternation. As a second year student, I can feel my ratings rise among the upper class students, many of whom make it a point to come and wish me a happy holiday and give me their phone numbers.

As we make our way back to the car, we take all the attention in stride, but as soon as the last door is shut, we break into laughter. My brothers promptly take the phone numbers out of my hands— rewards for getting up so early on their holiday. Two of the phone numbers find their way back to me. I read the names and shake my head, smiling. These guys are cold.

It has been a very good year for our family. My father's promotion to Director of Caltex Oil, Uganda, comes with a beautiful two story house in the exclusive suburb of Kololo. We have arrived. Now my friends will be impressed, especially now that I am thirteen and need to score points with the Cabinet Minister's son who lives in the same suburb. Most important, though, is the doctor's son who will be at a much-anticipated birthday party next Saturday. "Who's Who" of the mid to late teens will be there. Many students studying abroad are arranging their holidays around it. It is to be a 'see' and 'be seen' affair.

The holidays have begun. We have a whole month of freedom before we have to return to our respective boarding schools. The first week flies by. The usually quiet house is bustling with noise. Quite a bit of time of my time is spent figuring out what I am going to wear to the party, and talking to my friend, Caroline, on the telephone.

"How did you manage to get your parents to let you go?" she asks in amazement. My parents have a well deserved reputation for being strict. Many of my friends have heard my father preach at All Saints Church on several Sundays; they are well aware of his views on parties...especially where I am concerned.

"I'm going with my brothers, so it's okay," I reply, hoping my parents will think so, too, when I finally ask them. "How did you convince yours?" I ask because this is still Africa and thirteen-year-old girls do not just run off to parties regardless of their parents' religious persuasion, or lack thereof.

"They're out of town," she squeals. "And since my brother is looking after me, he's going to take me to the party if I promise not to tell."

I hate her. I can't believe her luck. I ponder the possibility of my parents going out Saturday night. It's time to exercise my own version of heathen prayer— the kind that has nothing to do with God, and everything to do with luck.

Saturday is finally here. It is another beautiful morning in Uganda. The temperature is the usual seventy-five degrees. My brothers are giving me a driving lesson in my mother's car, but I can't concentrate. I'm beginning to doubt whether my parents will let me go to the party. Besides that, my brothers are discussing the party and the girls they hope will be there. I realize these 'boy talks' are beginning to bother me. They are talking about girls as though they are mere conquests. After they are conquered, they are shifted into second place and the game begins again. I wonder how they keep track of them all?

Until now, their banter has not bothered me; I have been one of them. In their hand-me-downs, I've looked like them, down to the closely-cropped hair. I've even acted as a decoy on several occasions and averted messy encounters. Now I wonder if my boyfriends will talk about me like that? Will I be just another conquest to somebody? Just one piece in a five or ten piece jigsaw puzzle? Was the doctor's son, underneath all that sensitivity and sweet innocence, just another bag of testosterone on the prowl? My mind returns to the serious matter facing me. How am I going to talk my parents into letting me go to the party?

"No!" is my father's very definite reply as he peers at me over his cup of tea.

"But Daddy, why not? I'll be with Edward, Albert and Philip. They'll take care of me." I look around the table for support from my brothers. Not wanting to jeopardize their own chances, they busy themselves with their tea and leave me to fend for myself. "They're boys. They're different," is the reply.

I have just about had it with that answer. Ever since I have been asking to go out with my brothers, I've been denied on the charges that girls were different from boys. When did the rules change? I can still pack a mean punch, outplay them in tennis, hold my own in soccer, climb trees, hunt pheasant and swim. My only sister is just three years old and I'm always left behind with her and my two younger brothers while the three older boys go off and have fun. It just isn't fair.

I lose interest in my tea and sit sullenly staring at the table in front of me. My younger brother asks if I'm going to eat my bread. Getting no reply, he reaches over and helps himself. Nobody understands. Caroline's going to laugh at me, and the doctor's son will probably find someone else. I can't believe I'm not going. Suddenly my ears perk up. I can't believe what I'm hearing. My mother is telling the cook to give us supper and put us to bed. They are going out to a business dinner. I maintain my cool, but my heart is thumping. Yes! There is a God after all. I pretend to read a book on the sofa until the car is safely out of the gates...then I dart to my room.

"Where are you going?" Philip asks as I follow them out to the car later.

"I promise I won't tell Daddy that you took me. Please. I'll find someone to bring me back early."

They don't like it one bit, and I don't blame them. If Daddy were to ever find out that they had taken me to the party, they'd probably have to run out of town. Nobody who aided in the delinquency of Daddy's little girl was likely to be treated with kindness. Besides, they didn't want to spend their evening looking after me, or conversely, have me watch them. After some pleading (more like plea bargaining), they reluctantly agree and away we go.

I gear myself up for the grand entrance. I place myself strategically between my brothers. The party boy himself opens the door and welcomes us in. The house is beautifully decorated.

I spot Caroline immediately. We wave at each other briefly from across the large living room. As minors at this 'grown up' party, we have to maintain our cool. I check out the new pant-suit she's been talking about all week. It's alright. The one I'm wearing is better; it's a designer original. A birthday present from my mother.

Caroline watches me soak up the attention as we slowly make our way through the house, my brothers greeting friends they haven't seen in a while. We get to the door leading to the garden.

There are lights around the trees outside where many guests are taking advantage of the pleasant evening breeze. My brothers make a condition that I stay inside so they can keep an eye on me, then proceed to shake me off and disappear. As I walk back to the living room to find Caroline, I am stopped by a gentle touch on my shoulder. It's him, the doctor's son! My heart almost stops beating. My knees go into high support gear as I lose all sense of feeling for a few seconds.

"Can I have this dance?" He looks so handsome; all I can do is nod. He takes my hand and leads me onto the dance floor.

The evening passes by in a daze. He hardly lets go of my hand on and off the floor. Suddenly, I'm shocked back into reality. Panicked cries ring out, "Mr. Wilson! Mr. Wilson!" I see everyone straighten up as a tall man walks through the house looking for a young girl who wants the earth to open up and swallow her. My father zeroes in on his subject, looking neither left nor right. He takes me by the arm and calmly leads me out, looking neither left nor right. I look straight down.

The ride back home is very tense. There is an impregnable wall of silence. I can't even imagine what's going through his mind. One thing is for sure, there is no way out of this one. The ten-minute ride seems like an eternity, but finally we arrive and I meekly follow my father into the house. I count all twelve steps of the stairs that bring us into the living room.

The house is very quiet. My father goes up the three additional steps that lead to the dining room and heads straight to my mother's crystal cabinet. I stand nervously in the semi-darkness of the living room and watch my father select a magnificent glass, one of a set of six my mother had coveted from the moment she laid eyes on them in one of her women's magazines. She had finally managed to have them sent to her from London and they were her pride and joy. From where I stand, I can see the glass sparkle as my father holds it up to the light.

"Do you see this?" he asks, looking directly into my eyes.

I hold my breath and nod. He pauses for a split second, then opens his fingers. The glass crashes to the floor breaking into a million pieces. My eyes grow wide, my mouth falls open. My father is now watching me piercingly, making sure I have registered the seriousness of his action. Our eyes lock.

"That's your life. You drop it once and you'll never be able to put it back together again." With that he walks into the kitchen, leaving me alone to contemplate the little pieces strewn all over the dining room floor. He returns with a broom in one hand and a pan in the other.

"Now, go to your room and think about it."

Reflections - 22 years later

Many years after that poor glass met its demise, I found out that it was easy to win tennis championships at Lugogo Stadium, it was easy to play piano recitals at the National Theater, it was also fairly easy to remain 'unshattered' in the innocence of Africa, but it was next to impossible to hang tough in an America gone sex crazy. I know that I was a source of great joy in my father's life, but I was also a source of great pain.

Recently I happened to flip to one of these television talk shows and the subject caught my attention. Teenage sex. It caught my attention because I was writing this chapter of the book. I was amazed at how the hostess responded to a brave young girl in the audience who stood up and said she wasn't going to repeat her mother's mistakes, because her mother had taken the time to teach her and warn her of the consequences of those choices.

"But isn't it true that by your mother telling you she had sex before marriage she's only giving you permission to do it because she did it?" the hostess asked her. Then before giving the young lady a chance to respond, she walked away.

This is not the first time I have been shocked at some of the asinine deductions people make from perfectly good truth. We learn from our mistakes; if not from ours, then those of others, if we are smart. What was that mother supposed to do? Lie to her daughter? Hide from her past at the expense of letting her daughter repeat the same mistakes?

> *"Virtuous men do good by setting themselves up*
> *as models before the public, but I do good*
> *by setting myself up as a warning."*
>
> Michael de Montaigne

Of all the wonderful virtues my father possessed, the one I most admired and respected was his honesty, his ability to "walk in the Light" with graciousness and love. With his example still ringing clearly in my heart and mind, I wish only to more and more develop this virtue in me. We are on the path towards an intelligent Christianity that will give us a fresh vision for a new humanity. We can't do it unless we walk in the Light...the Light of God, with graciousness and truth. I, like Mr. Montaigne, hope to do good by setting myself up as a warning.

There are many people who say they don't regret anything they have done in their lives, and I envy them. I know that my path has been necessary for my development, and I also know that my radical departure from Christ was also a springboard for my radical return. However, I have a regret, and if I could go back I would not let the crystal glass slip out of my hand. It was a one-of-a-kind, designer original, and I broke it and cast my pearls before swines. Jesus heals us, makes us whole, gives us peace in our souls, but He does not erase the memories.

I know now that had Jesus Christ been the Lord of my life, I would not have gone the way I did. But without Him, what hope did I have to withstand the missiles that were leveled at me to destroy me? I am proof that having good breeding and good, loving, Christian parents is not enough. We need to accept Christ for ourselves to win at this game called life. I am grateful to God that even after we do a jig with the pigs, He draws us back into His loving arms, mud and all. He specializes in 'after shatter' clean-up because so many of us insist on meeting Him after rather than before.

It is important not to dwell on our past because it can be a source of discouragement, but life is a process of building precept upon precept. We are building on those pasts. If they were good we draw strength and courage from them. If they were bad, they cripple us until we seek for healing from Jesus and move on to build on His Foundation. Then can we set out guideposts for others.

Welcome to America

I first left Uganda in 1974. I was sixteen and a half. The euphoria that had accompanied Idi Amin's takeover in 1971 had turned to despair as Amin's maniacal rule of terror plunged our beautiful country into a nightmare of unfathomable proportions. The country that Sir Winston Churchill had dubbed the "Pearl of Africa" was well on its way to becoming the "Killing Fields of Africa."

People disappeared every day. There was a shortage of essential commodities. Rumours of Idi Amin's notorious torture chambers had everyone petrified of being seen in town. When husbands left for work in the morning their families were never sure they would see them again that evening. Roadblocks manned by uneducated, trigger-happy gunmen were set up all over the country. It was a time in Uganda's history when a watch was worth more than a human life. I remember it as a dark time.

As in most cases of exile, our exit was under pressure. My father could smell his coffee burning. The main target groups were the Christians (Amin wanted to make Uganda into a Moslem state), the Baganda (Uganda's largest and most dominant ethnic group), and the educated elite (the influential who fueled Amin's insecurities). My father was all three. Of course, my siblings and I were thrilled when we found out we were going to America.

As the British Airways Boeing 707 pulled away from the terminal, I looked at the crowd that had braved their way through the road blocks to come and see us off. Daniel, the doctor's son, stood a few feet away from the rest. He was heart-broken. We had become inseparable. It is very probable that had I stayed in Uganda I would have married him. As it was, I would not see Daniel again for six years. We promised to write each other every day.

I will always remember landing at Kennedy airport on a hot August evening. As my parents fussed with our baggage, my younger siblings and I were awestruck by the size of the cars that pulled into and out of the loading zones. Somehow, everything in America seemed to be built on a larger scale. Even the people seemed a bit larger...and they were all in such a great hurry to get somewhere. We stood in the middle of the airport amazed. My father, the seasoned traveler, laughed at us.

"You all look like you were raised on a farm," he teased.

It is quite curious that during the week we spent on the East Coast before heading for California, we saw everything from the Empire State Building to the Statue of Liberty, we travelled to Boston and Philadelphia and saw Liberty Bells and heard about tea parties, but nowhere did we see the streets of gold that America was fabled to possess. In fact, parts of New York were downright scary, not to mention the scenes that met our unbelieving eyes as we cruised through Harlem.

California, on the other hand, shared similarities with the Kenyan coastal town of Mombasa. Palm trees swayed gently in the wind. And the heat! I remember being engulfed in billows of warm air as we stepped out of the air-conditioned airport building. My younger brother stood wide-eyed as he viewed the scantily dressed natives. Here, people were more relaxed, they seemed friendlier, but it soon became quite obvious that Americans, on the whole, were most uninformed about Africa. To them, Africans still lived in the bush.

A month after our arrival, I found myself a senior at a private Christian high school with a total black population of four— and one of them was my brother, who was a freshman. You can imagine my dismay at finding out I was the only black girl in the whole school. It was no wonder I did Disneyland solo on grad night.

During that year there was a rumour that a certain senior girl was having an affair with a teacher. I was horrified. Then another girl was quietly sent away to an unmarried mother's home in another state. I couldn't believe it. The little Miss Goody Two Shoes that I was, often recoiled at the level of intimacy my fellow students displayed in public. It was improper. I missed my Daniel. I longed for the atmosphere of relative innocence we still enjoyed in Africa. Our love had been sweet and pure.

After a year in California my family moved to Kenya. I was left behind to go to college. A 'good' college, a 'safe' college. Somehow I was not surprised when I found myself at a Christian college, and although the percentage of black students was a little higher, my choices were not. The available black men were older and more serious. I, on the other hand, was approaching my eighteenth birthday and seeking to make up for the boring, dateless year I had just spent in high school. Being a full-blooded female, the lack of eligible, young black men did not erase my need for a relationship with the opposite sex and it was only a matter of time before I was having crushes on young, equally full-blooded white collegiates.

My college experience was quickly soured by the overt racism I experienced from some of the students and professors. A sad commentary on Christianity. Besides, I was majoring in piano, working towards a classical music degree. What on earth was Africa going to do with a classical pianist? Africa needed communication experts.

Armed with a new major, I applied and was accepted into the University of Southern California's School of Cinema and Television Production. I forced my way out of the protective barriers my wonderful parents had placed me in and entered into a side of America that was sad, lonely and empty. I was at USC. The University of Spoiled Children. Children with a lot of money, and very little love and guidance.

I was on my own. I had no one to tell me when to eat. I had no curfews. There were no laws against drinking or smoking. I did not need to profess to be anything I wasn't. I was free to do with my body whatever I wished. This, I had always thought, was paradise. What I had not bargained for was the moral and social disorder I found among the American youth. I ran into a couple of my classmates outside a class one morning. One was crumpled on the floor holding her stomach, the other trying to comfort her. I rushed over to see if I could help and was told confidentially by the friend that the girl had just had an abortion, all she needed to do was go back home and rest up.

I remember thinking what a dirty girl she was...she had done the 'naughty' thing. I was nineteen then. It was not long, however, before the environment, coupled with the sheer need for companionship, led me into some of the most frightening years of my life. It is true when they say that Americans are friendly, but they don't make good friends. It is also true that this is one of the loneliest societies in the world. I became very lonely. Before too long I was forced to lower my standards in order to fit in. The more I compromised, the further I drifted from my Christian foundation, the more calloused I became. By the time I was twenty, I had shattered crystal for a life.

My experience with the world was not done in rebellion against my parents; no one loved her parents more. They had tried to talk me out of transferring to a secular university, but in the end they respected my decision, and I appreciated the sacrifices they made to support me. My father made all the provisions he could to ensure my safety; from finding Christian guardians for me (George and Dorothy Smoker who were parents to me in every way), to getting scholarships to cover the outrageous school fees

(I am most grateful to the Elizabeth Whitsett Foundation for their gracious support).

My father was unhappy that I would have to work to pay my rent, but with seven children and five of them college age, he couldn't do it. I didn't want him to. This was my decision, and he had already done everything he could, short of going without salt. I was declaring my independence. I wanted to work, to live in the real world.

Living in an inner city area just south of the campus, I was exposed to a way of life my friends in Africa would never believe. I can only attribute my survival to the Lord God whose love endures forever, and who does not abandon the works of His hands. At one point I became so disillusioned with life I wanted out. I was tired of supping at the trough, but too proud to admit defeat. It would have been easy to find someone on the street desperate enough to do me in for a couple of hundred dollars...and I thought about it long and hard.

My story is of the twentieth century prodigal. The scriptures had commanded my parents to bring up their children in the 'discipline and instruction of the Lord' (Ephesians 6:4), a..d they had. Right before that, however, the scriptures had laid out some instructions for me in Ephesians 6:1-3.

"CHILDREN, obey your parents in the Lord, for this is right. HONOUR YOUR FATHER AND MOTHER (which is the first commandment with a promise), THAT IT MAY BE WELL WITH YOU, AND THAT YOU MAY LIVE LONG ON THE EARTH." (NASB translation)

The above verses are typed exactly as they are found in the Bible, capital letters and all. I want to challenge you to go through the Bible and read only the capitalized words and sentences. Then I want you to do as they say. You will be amazed to find that these are the TRUTHS of LIFE. These are the keys that open the door to God's heart.

I didn't read my Bible much after I left the security of a

Christian environment with all its rules and regulations. I didn't take the lesson of the crystal glass with me when I finally faced the world alone. I didn't do as my parents taught me. I took my eyes off Jesus. Instead, I tried to prove that women could do whatever men did, and as each one of my premises fell, I clung onto another. I tried to find fulfillment in school, then in human beings, then in pot, then in sex, then in the pursuit of fame and fortune. I was trying to find happiness from the outside in. All the while pretending I was having fun.

Throughout it all, my parents prayed for me. They had put me in the only place they could— in the hands of God, and they kept me there— daily. They trusted God's Word which promised them that if they brought their children up in the way in which they should go, even if they went off the deep end for a while, eventually they would come to their senses. If they stayed out there long enough, eventually they would end up in the pigpen, and those who had been taught their value as children of God would find the strength and the courage to put aside their foolish pride and return to God...return to fulfill their potential as children of THE KING, holy and acceptable.

I am more than grateful to God that He 'hemmed me in— behind and before' (Psalm 139:5), and kept me safe through those turbulent years. I am grateful that He didn't allow me to get all manner of diseases even though my behaviour certainly warranted it. In the late seventies, early eighties, American society was on a rapid downward spiral. The flower movement and the sexual revolution was coming to fruition and along with it came diseases too horrible to mention. Today, in the nineties, the minefield is so dense that if you listen to the world and take your eyes off Jesus, and off the lessons your Godly parents are trying to teach you, you may not only break the glass...you may die!

Chapter 4

Screams in the Wilderness

I'll always remember the brilliance of the African sunrise along the eastern coast of Kenya as we prepared to land at Jomo Kenyatta International Airport. I felt a desire to kneel down and kiss the soil, to let my mother Africa know I was home, that I had survived America. I had thought and dreamt about this moment so often, and now as I looked around the airport, at the African people going to and fro, the emotions gripping me were so powerful there was no holding them back. Mother Africa welcomed me back to herself in an embrace that assured me that no matter where my travels took me, Africa was and would always be my home.

I remember crying as I fell into my mother's open arms. I grabbed my brothers and sister and gave them each fierce hugs. I thought I had died and gone to little, African-girl heaven. Little did I know that my return after six years in the concrete jungles of Los Angeles was going to be more of a culture shock than my first experience with America. My grandfather hated the American accent that now flavoured my speech; I would have to get used to living under my father's roof again, for in Africa, a girl leaves home only when she gets married. My siblings had grown up and weren't quite sure what to make of this person who had come back to invade their territory. And we were still living in exile outside our beloved Uganda.

With my father's connections, I got a chance to produce and direct some shows on the Voice of Kenya television. It was a thrill to see my name roll up on the screen on national television. It was my validation to my peers who thought I had wasted four years in college just to read the news on television. A degree in Cinema/Television Production was a little obscure for some of my aunts. I also gained credibility in my sister's eyes when I brought some of the television stars home for tea. She would get on the phone and call up all of her friends.

"They're here! They're sitting right in my living room!"

But...there was something missing. I had flirted with Hollywood, been enticed by a hedonistic society, and had lost my innocence. A ten o'clock curfew for a twenty-two-year-old who had lived on her own for much of the past five years was a pill hard to swallow. My father's response to my requests for leniency was, "What is there to do out there after ten o'clock except get into trouble? If you want to visit with your friends after ten o'clock bring them here." For what? The proverbial English 'tea and a natter?' That was done at five o'clock.

Careerwise, I was driven by the need to be rich and famous, but the scripts I submitted to the Voice of Kenya for half/hour series were continually being rejected. "Too American." "African girls wouldn't do that." "No holding hands on local television." Soon, unable to find opportunities to express my semi-African/semi-American self, I applied (with my father's encouragement and support) to graduate school in California.

Spiritually, I was searching. After many bitter experiences with racism in America, I was sure I could never find myself in the 'white' man's religion and, therefore, totally rejected Christianity. I had come back to Africa determined to look into traditional African religions. I also called around to find somewhere that would teach me about transcendental meditation. I had such a driven personality, I needed an anchor. I needed something to believe in. My father had told me many times, "Always have something you believe in enough to die for." I had a place inside me that was thirsty...that needed to be touched, but I never quite seemed to find the answer.

While waiting for a reply from California, I had opportunities to drive into Uganda several times with my father on some of his relief missions. In the drought-stricken areas of the north, particularly in Karamoja, I saw scenes of human suffering that became indelibly etched into my memory forever. Little children too weak to pick themselves up out of their excrement. The foul smell of human hopelessness covered camps, and camps of people just waiting to die. And it was not their fault. They hadn't asked for the drought. They hadn't asked for Idi Amin. They hadn't asked for the rebels to come and steal their cattle and chase them out of their homes.

I left those camps totally discouraged. Where was this God that was supposed to be loving and caring? I didn't understand His behaviour. It didn't seem very Godly at all to have all these people starving to death. What had they done to deserve it? Especially the children. How could He bear to see them suffer like that? I usually had no urge to eat, and my father had to remind me that without my strength I was no good to them.

Then I saw my father. Hauling bags of porridge, sweating in small, smoky school kitchens across that area showing the teachers how to prepare breakfast for their little pupils whose only hope for food every day was what my father was providing through the Christian organization he worked with. On the special trips when my mother could come with us, I saw them take turns stirring the heavy ladle and dishing out the sweet, nutrient-packed porridge into the bowls. I would then have the privilege of handing bowls of nourishment to expectant, hopeful, little faces. I would sit and watch them eating with such joy and gratitude, each a beautiful miracle of the African spirit and a testament to our future. A future they would possibly not have had if my father had not intervened.

I knew that something special drove my parents to love children over and beyond their own seven children, but I didn't want to believe it was their love for Jesus. I knew many people who professed the love of Christ, but I didn't see them out there. Little did I know then that they were instilling in me the sense of joyful duty and service to those who were less fortunate than we. It was as simple as affirming one's right to eat and live in peace with their families. Many have said that my father came into his own when he stood at the pulpit to preach, but I think he came into his own when he was surrounded by scores of well-fed children who could now delight in his stories of Jesus without their tummies grumbling.

Then we would drive through miles and miles of pure beauty. The Ugandan landscape is indeed a testimony to a Creator with a love for beauty and elegance. Vast plains of land bathed in bright sunlight for miles and miles. Every so often we would see a group of gazelles, a giraffe in the distance, and an assorted variety of animals grazing here and there. For a few moments, I would forget the pain and suffering of the refugee camps and my mind would be caught up in the magic of Africa. But more often than not, those moments would come to a screeching halt as we ran into instant roadblocks. I would find myself staring straight down the barrel of an AK-47; a few feet behind it was always a face uglier than the one before.

These were the realities of my beloved Africa, and when I returned to America to embark on a graduate degree in Third World Film, I carried with me the pain of Africa's helplessness against the forces that were tearing her apart. I also carried with me a new purpose - to gain power...as much power as it would take to free her! This I was ready to die for.

I credit UCLA for restoring my faith in universities. Here I was able to spend time with my professors. The students were real people, and I made many good friends of substance. The African Studies Department fueled my 'coming of conscious' mind. I was exposed to thinkers and revolutionaries like Franz Fanon, Walter Rodney and Jomo Kenyatta. Ousmane Sembene, the father of

African film, became my idol. Minoring in African literature, I spent much of my time exploring the minds of our literary greats like Wole Soyinka and Lewis Nkosi.

I saw films with titles like *Black God, White Devil.* I debated the issues of social injustice with my schoolmates and friends, many who came from varying countries in Africa. We made a pact to rewrite the dictionary and stop Webster from defining our realities. We sought to eliminate words like 'Third World' because as far as we were concerned there was only one world... and we were all living in it.

Meanwhile, Ugandans were continuing to die in the hundreds of thousands. Innocent victims caught in the war between the military government of Milton Obote, and his opponent the popular resistance leader, Yoweri Museveni. I would sit in front of the television and weep as picture after picture tore at my heart. Everyone was suffering. No one was exempt. Death crept through the Luweero Triangle slaying men, women and children, leaving behind ghost towns.

I channeled my helplessness into school. When my grades came back that first quarter I had made all A's. A clean 4.0. One big guy in my class made the unfortunate remark that I didn't look like an A student to him. As I contemplated his fate, I learned he had made less than a B average. I smiled smugly and forgave him. Both beauty and brains had escaped this poor fellow; how could I be mad at him?

On the surface, everything seemed to be going my way. I had a nice, little apartment in a much brighter neighbourhood. I was offered a scholarship from UCLA which covered my nonresident tuition. My older brother bought a small car for me, turning my one hour bus ride to school into a ten-minute trip. I was in an exciting relationship with a young German jetsetter who lived in Berlin but spent quite a bit of time in Los Angeles. I was well on my way to showing everybody what I was made of.

But...it wasn't enough. I wanted more, and I wanted it as soon as possible. School seemed to be taking up too much time, time I could use to make money. So, I quit school. After all, I already had one degree. The little girl from Africa was going to make it big, first by modeling and acting, then producing and directing my own movies. She had it all planned out. She was going to drive a smoky blue Jaguar XJS convertible.

I managed to get an agent and we sat down to map out a strategy. There were pictures to be taken, composites to be made, resumes to print. Then came the interviews. Interview after interview. "Sorry, business is bad for blacks; try again next year." "You don't have the look we're looking for." What look was that? "We don't know." "Lose five pounds and come back." I was 5' 9" and weighed 120 pounds— five pounds would have put me in with the living dead.

Sometimes I would get the job; many times I didn't. Hollywood wasn't opening up as fast as I had planned, but nevertheless I remained optimistic. After all, in this business, sometimes it took years. The secret was persistence and determination. I marched in and out of interviews with "persistence and determination" ringing in my head. Sometimes I walked out of the office and did a jig. Other times, most times, I would hold my head up proudly and walk out determined to show them.

It was not long before my misery found company. I met a young black American model at an interview and we struck up an instant friendship. We were both discouraged with the way our dreams were crumbling around us. We would notice how most of the other girls were driving snappy little sports cars and moving in circles we could only dream of. The more we saw the discrepancies between their lives and ours, the more discontented we became. Why didn't we have those things, the nice apartments, the invitations to the 'happening parties', the nice cars, the extra money? These girls weren't particularly better looking than we were, and in some cases even being white couldn't help them out.

Of course...it didn't take a genius to figure it out...sugar daddies. We looked at each other and the lights went on in our pea-brains (or, in this case, the lights went out). That's what we needed! Sugar daddies. Who would ever know? Her parents lived in another state, mine were half way around the world. When I was with her the idea sounded great, but when I was alone the idea stunk. My parents did not raise me to become what I was thinking about becoming.

I agonized over the turn of events, but the more I thought about my raggedy little Volkswagen the more I rationalized it. It would just be like having a rich boyfriend. But my father's warm brown eyes kept coming into the picture. He was so proud of me; how could I do this to him? The angrier I became over Africa's ills, the more it became simply a matter of ethics. I would just have a short relationship with a very rich man, get enough money to give my career a boost, then I'd go solo. Was this the kind of role model I wanted to be for my sister? Even if no one ever found out, even if it was just for one day, even if I corrected all of Africa's woes, would I be able to live with the memory?

Finally, I decided sugar daddies just didn't fall out of the sky so there was no use agonizing over it. There was only one problem, I didn't take into account how very interested the devil was in my struggle. I didn't believe in a devil. In fact, I was embarking on the most anti-Christian campaign of my life. I was a modern day Saul, out to destroy Christianity. I remember those parties with my UCLA friends, eating, drinking wine, sometimes smoking weed, intellectualizing, discussing politics, and cursing the white man and his Christian God for our oppression and confusion. It just didn't make sense in my mind that my parents— two of the most beautiful, wonderful, intelligent, well-educated, well-traveled human beings— believed in that blond, blue-eyed Jesus. How could they be so blind?

I continued on with my interviews and one day, as I walked out onto Wilshire Boulevard in Beverly Hills, I almost bumped into an older gentleman. Thinking nothing of it, I excused myself and went on to my car. At the very first light, just as the signal was about to change, the car next to me honked. I ignored it and started towards the next light. Again the honk. I quickly glanced over and my eyes almost fell out of my sockets. There was this beautiful, silver-gray Rolls Royce, and sitting in the back seat, smiling at me, was the gentleman I had almost knocked over. I smiled weakly and quickly looked away.

The next signal light was red. Again the honk. This time I was being signaled to pull over. My mind went into shock. "I can't," I told myself, but a little voice inside said, "What will it hurt? Just go with the flow. Have a little fun." I looked over, and he signaled again. I became bold and turned down the next street and parked. The Rolls Royce parked behind me. The chauffeur got out and made his way to my car.

"The gentleman in the car would like to speak to you."

"Can't he speak for himself?" I asked the white chauffeur, trying to hang on to a false sense of pride.

The man left and went back to the car. I watched nervously through the rearview mirror. He opened the car door and bent over to relay my message. The gentleman stepped out, smiling, probably amused at the nerve coming from one who drove such a car. This time I noticed how immaculately dressed he was...and how old. Not wanting him to come too close to my car, I stepped out and met him halfway. What in the world was I supposed to do? Be yourself, I told myself. But the 'me' I knew wanted to run. I didn't know the one that wanted to stay.

We quickly dispensed with the greetings, and I waited for his next move. I looked into his pale blue eyes, surrounded by two semi-circles of wrinkles which extended down his cheek when he smiled.

"I was wondering if we could get together sometime?"

I had to think fast. He was old, but not repulsive. I looked away, ashamed of what I was about to say.

"If it's mutually profitable," I blurted out.

"That goes without saying," he replied. I felt stupid. We exchanged phone numbers.

I drove away feeling cheap. I had a chance to be intelligent, to show my first-class upbringing; instead, I had put myself up for sale. I felt like I was about to shatter whatever bits and pieces of my crystal glass I had managed to salvage. And for what? Money! The root of all evil, so says the Bible. Not in itself, of course, but certainly my attitude towards it was fertile ground for all manner of negative behaviour.

I began to remember, much against my will, some of the lessons my father and mother had taught me. "If you are going to sell your soul to the devil make sure you get it all...the house, the car, the million dollars. Take the highest bid," my father had said in one of his sermons. "But what does it profit a man to gain the whole world, and forfeit his soul?" Mark 8:36.

That stuff was garbage, I told myself, just a bunch of hogwash. The missionaries had come to Africa with a Bible in one hand and a gun in the other. How could I believe and worship a God like that? Give me Jah. Now this was a God for black people. A God who would understand my need to free my people...by any means necessary. I didn't need that "nailed to the cross for my sins" business. I couldn't get into that effeminate, blond, blue-eyed man I saw hanging in the pictures. He looked pathetic.

Mr. Money Bags wasted no time getting in touch with me. We set up a date for lunch...to get to know one another, and to lay our cards on the table. I took meticulous care to look my Beverly Hills best, got into my green Volkswagen and drove off. I was going to be cool, real cool. As I sat across the table from this man who was a good fifteen years older than my father, I felt as though I was in a "dreammare." What was I doing here? I felt like the women in this fancy restaurant were looking at me with contempt, and the men were looking at me as though I was lunch. I didn't belong there. At least not in this capacity.

We talked about this and that. I found out he owned a string of theaters across the nation. He found out I was a student/struggling model/actress/director/producer, etc. He also found that I lived in a part of town he and his Rolls Royce could not be seen in.

"We're going to have to do something about that, aren't we? And that car, too." He said matter-of-factly.

I almost choked on my food. Show time! My dream car, my dream apartment were being handed to me on a golden platter. I smiled feebly. Something hit a very wrong nerve. There had to be a better way. He casually pulled out a thick roll of new, crisp, one-hundred-dollar bills. I had never seen so much money in my life. I tried to act nonchalant. He pulled one out and folded it neatly beside my plate. I looked around to see if anyone had seen him do it, then looked straight down at my plate.

"Just a little token to show you I mean business. I really like you, my little African intellect." Money, endearments, private number...already? Had I officially joined the ranks of the 'kept'?

That was Thursday. We were set up to meet the following Tuesday. I went home to begin the most agonizing weekend of my life. This time I was going to prove my end of the bargain. Friday I was listless all day. Everything had turned sour. My model friend turned a darker shade of chocolate from envy mixed with excitement. All she could think of were the cool parties we would have at my new apartment, and cruising around in my sports car. All I could think of was the crystal glass. This time I saw myself irretrievably shattering the remaining pieces with a huge baseball bat. This was my life we were talking about, not a replaceable piece of man-made glass.

Saturday I was tired. I had spent a sleepless night trying to work out a deal with the devil. How much was my soul worth? Was I guaranteed happiness and was life going to be one big party? Would my parents drive the his and hers Mercedeses I was planning to buy them in peace? Or would my father's acute spiritual antennae reveal to him that they were fruits from the devil's orchard? Somehow, the party had gone out of my life.

At the time, my father worked with an evangelistic organization that sent African evangelists around the world preaching the word of God. On occasion, there were particular sermons they needed transcribed from tape to print. Since the African accent was difficult for the American secretaries to understand, I was asked to help. This had proven to be an effective way to make extra money during my school days, but it had now turned into an irritation. Not that I couldn't use the money, I just didn't want to hear about God.

However, to keep myself busy that day, I pulled out a tape and plopped it into the cassette player. I kept thinking to myself after Tuesday I would never have to type these boring sermons again. It so happened that I chose a tape of a sermon given by a white South African evangelist called Michael Cassidy. You can imagine how I despised white South Africans. I wanted to put them all in one giant incinerator and flick the switch myself. Everything Michael Cassidy had to say that day was met with pure, unadulterated, black African venom. I called him names not to be found in the Bible.

The last time I remembered feeling so low, so empty, so suicidal had been at USC. I didn't want to go through that again. So why was I feeling so empty, so angry, so frustrated? If confidence was to be found in the flesh, I had everything. I had arrived. And my 'keeper' was so old, he didn't need more than just a warm, young body to cuddle with every now and then. Sex, if at all, would be more the exception than the norm. Still...the thought of that leathery old skin rubbing next to mine was sickening.

The Jesus stuff I was listening to was making me sick, too, so I decided to get dressed, go find a party, get high and celebrate my good fortune. However, I was too ashamed to see anyone. By nine o'clock that evening, I was feeling so wound up, so caged in, I got into my car and drove onto the freeway screaming at the top of my lungs. I wanted to shout the pain out, to reach the inner recesses of my heart and find the answer. I drove to Santa Monica and back, pushing that poor Volkswagen at full throttle. I was crying out for help. Could anyone hear me? Did anyone care?

Maybe if I had stopped screaming for a few seconds I would have heard the gentle voice from above telling me how very much He cared, how He wanted to make it all go away if I would just stop running long enough to give Him a chance. But I kept on running.

On the way home I stopped off at a supermarket and loaded up on all my favourite foods. Ice cream, cantaloupes, junk and junk. I was tired of watching what I ate. Why did I have to look like a refugee to get work? I went home and stuffed my face, but that idea backfired in a bad way; I became so sick I found myself crawling to the bathroom for relief. I tried the television, the radio, reading, then decided to finish transcribing Michael's tape.

"There's a gap in everybody's life which can only be filled by God." The words came at me in that familiar English accent. I knew Michael Cassidy personally. He was one of my father's best friends, and I liked him. He was a good man despite being South African. I knew that whatever he had to say was true, and right then he seemed like he was talking to me. "Victoria, there's a gap in your life, an emptiness you're trying to fill. You cannot put anything in that gap except God. You have tried everything else...why don't you give God a chance?"

I turned the tape recorder off and walked away. God pulled me back to the chair and sat me down. I saw my hand reach for the machine and press the button. "Human beings were made for communion with God, that's what the gap is for." I sat back thinking of Tuesday. I tried to bargain with God. "Not today, Lord. Wednesday. If I got one hundred dollars for lunch..." Michael's voice went on calmly, "Just as you cannot put a violin in a guitar case, or a guitar in a case made for a bass, neither can you put anything else in the place that belongs to God."

"That's enough. Forget this whole thing," I said, reaching out to turn off the player, but I found myself crying uncontrollably. I couldn't see to stop the machine, and Michael went on gently ushering me into the Kingdom of God. Here I was, Miss Cool, Miss Too-Tough-To-Cry, broken, crying tears like I had never cried before. I knew it was time to stop running. I could hear Him clearly. I looked up to heaven and said simply, "Lord, if You are there...and I don't believe You are, but if You are real then come in and fill the gap in my life. Make me whole."

In an instant, from one second to the next, I felt as though something snapped inside of me. The Lord knew that a hardhead like me needed a conversion experience like that to believe it was really He. No one can tell me it didn't happen. No one can take it away from me. There is nothing I could have smoked, snorted, injected, or swallowed that could have freed my soul like Jesus freed me on June 27, 1982, at 1:30 A.M. I jumped out of my chair and rushed to the bathroom. There, staring at me in the mirror, was the biggest smile I had seen on my face in a long time, and the tears just kept streaming down my cheeks. I was free. I could breathe. I could smile. I could laugh again. I felt good.

I thought I was dreaming. The depression that had been choking me was gone. It doesn't happen this way to everyone, but I'm sure glad it happened to me. I was afraid I would wake up the next morning and find myself empty again, but when I woke up I looked outside, and the sun was shining brighter than I had ever seen it. I stepped outside and the grass was greener, the air seemed fresher. I remembered my father saying that the night he accepted Jesus he had slept in a different place— in the arms of God. I, too, had slept in the arms of God.

I immediately called Nairobi.

"Daddy, Daddy, I'm born-again!" I heard the phone drop, and I could hear my father running around the house yelling that Victoria had accepted Jesus. My mother rushed to the phone.

"Victoria, is it true?"

"Yes. Last night. I was listening to a tape by Michael Cassidy and it all fell into place. I am born-again."

The next call was to Michael Cassidy in South Africa. He was ecstatic. My much-relieved brothers took me out to dinner to celebrate; my lifestyle had began to cause them great anxiety. Keeping me in line had been no easy task; they figured God would have a better chance.

Now it was time to sever my past. I had been given a fresh slate. Monday morning I dialed the private number. He picked up the phone and I told him I could not go through with our arrangement. He tried to talk me into giving it a chance.

"Have you found someone else? No one can give you what I can give you."

"I have found someone else, and He's given me eternal life."

When I look back now I marvel at God's timing. It is well said that God is never early, and He is never late, He is always right on time. He snatched me back just as the big claw was closing in on me. Anyone could have given me cars, apartments, money; I eventually would have done it for myself with persistence and determination, but at what cost to my soul? When Jesus said, "Friend, your sins are forgiven. Your faith has saved you, go in peace," He freed my soul and gave me back my life, my dignity, my self-respect.

For the first time I understood and believed for myself those words I had heard so often... God loves you and has a wonderful plan for your life.

Chapter 5

Standing in the Fire of Love

"You will know the Truth, and the Truth will make you free...so if the SON makes you free, you will be FREE INDEED."

Jesus · John 8:32,36

I had found the Truth. I was radically saved. So much so I re-enrolled at UCLA and set out to convert all my friends. I was in love with God. First love to the bone. I could now actually read the Bible and understand it. One of the few Christian friends I had came over and explained to me the plan of salvation. She drew the cute little picture that shows you where you are without Jesus, then how the cross brings you over to the other side. I listened politely.

Eventually, I concluded she had dismissed the thousands of times I had been to church, Bible studies, Scripture Union meetings, revival meetings, and Sunday school, so, I stopped her. I knew the Bible. I was, after all, my father's daughter. Every lesson he ever taught me was based on Biblical truth. I also had thirty college units of Bible under my belt, and had probably memorized every important verse in the Scriptures at one time or another. The devil hadn't stolen that from me, he had only blinded me for a season. Now my intellectual knowledge had become heart knowledge. Now all those concepts made sense. I felt them. I believed them. They became a part of me. I knew without a doubt that I had received the touch I had longed for in the innermost part of my being. My spirit had come alive.

I quickly looked up some Ugandan friends I knew and plugged into their church. This was a predominantly white church located near a beach community and it had a vision for the youth. Their services were upbeat, the worship was great, and it was a change to see the older members of the church clapping and praising God alongside their sons and daughters. I sat in wonder many times as young men and women gave themselves to Christ under the powerful teaching. I wondered why I had never been to a church like this before. Maybe I would have come to the Lord sooner and saved myself all the grief.

I wrote many letters to my father, and he wrote back teaching me, encouraging me. In one of his letters he wrote,

"We have known you all along since the very beginning, you have always been so close to my heart, you have always been a beautiful Electric Bulb and suddenly, the greatest thing has happened, LIGHT HAS COME INTO THE BULB, now no darkness can hide it anymore. We all pray that the Light will burn brighter and brighter and many will see it and glorify the Lord of our Salvation."

It seemed like I had walked into a ready-made relationship with my Father in Heaven. I was already familiar with His attributes of graciousness and loving kindness. I knew what pleased Him, I knew how to be in constant fellowship with Him. I knew I could trust Him with all my concerns. I knew He would take care of me and provide for me. I had seen and experienced it on a human level. I had heard my father many times from the pulpit, making comparisons between my relationship with him with our relationship with God. I was comfortable talking about my relationship with God and much of my early evangelism was centered around Him, but He was only one person in the Trinity. As I continued to go to church and fellowship with other young Christians, I realized I needed to come in touch with the other two persons of the Trinity, Jesus and the Holy Spirit.

Coming from a continent that lives in the spirit world, the

Holy Spirit wasn't too difficult to understand, particularly when He was explained to me as the Breath of God who had power over all the demonic forces that had my people under siege. That was great...I was ready to go declare war on the devil. Now I had the answer for Africa...the Holy Spirit of God.

Ironically, it was the fact that I was African and black that made Jesus a bit of an embarrassment. I had never seen a picture or image of God. I had my own special image of Him. But Jesus, in the picture on our living room wall at home, had long, silky smooth, golden brown hair. He had a delicate narrow nose, gentle blue eyes looking up to heaven, and a creamy complexion. He looked properly meek and mild in His robe, and white beyond a shadow of a doubt.

There have been two periods in my life that stand out as very unique. Times when I experienced two diametric emotions at the same time. One was to come later on when I grieved the death of my father at the same time I was falling in love with my husband. Now, as I sought to find a central place for Jesus in my life, I was also completing a Master's degree in 'black liberation.' One preached freedom through peace, the other freedom through violence if necessary. One preached surrender, the other power and control. One had a white face, the other— every shade of brown. One was theistic, the other humanistic.

I became conscious of omitting the name of Jesus in my philosophical debates with my classmates. I couldn't defend Him when it came to what the white race had done in the world. Yet I knew that if it hadn't been for Jesus and what He had done for me on that cross two thousand years ago, I would not have entered into the relationship with God that I now enjoyed. But how could I translate that into terminology my revolutionary comrades would not scorn as a bunch of colonialist nonsense? To them Christianity was still the opiate of the people because it kept them dependent and ignorant in regard to their real needs. The church was just another way to support the status quo, a denial of the oppressed people's sufficiency to create their own future. Not to mention the multitudes of Christian organizations that were using Africa's problems to support the American economy.

In a very real way, I knew they were right. I saw it. That my parents would have a picture of a white Jesus hanging in their living room was proof of subtle brainwashing, a quiet, but wholesale acceptance of the lie that Jesus was white. The missionaries had done good things, on the whole, but their comrades in arms were wretched. They destroyed our self-worth, and trampled all over our dignity. They exploited us under every yoke imaginable to man. If all the record books from both sides were balanced, what was stolen from Africa outweighed the foreign debt one million to one. You could not put a price on our fathers, our mothers, our sisters and brothers, only our silver, and gold, and diamonds, and copper, and ivory, and...and. And the so-called world 'trade' was still desperately skewed against us.

Yet, despite my anger towards white people, I couldn't allow it to keep me away from a relationship with Jesus. I needed to really study Jesus for myself, to take off the blinders man had put on me and see Jesus for who He really was. Before I could tell my fellow Africans that Jesus was the only solution to our health problems, to our hunger problems, to our relational problems, to our debt problems, to our self-governance problems, to our freedom problems...I needed to be convinced. I needed to know Jesus, to know His heart and put mine in sync with His.

The first thing I did was study the Jewish people of Jesus' time, and I saw that they were a cross between brown and olive in complexion. That fascinated me. I believe God, in His divine wisdom, predestined Jesus to be born a Jew because Jesus in human form had been neither black, or white, or red, or yellow. His hair was neither straight or curly. He had been a perfect blend of all.

I grabbed onto that concept and started preaching from a 'Jesus-was-a-brown-man' pulpit. I tried to enlighten my brothers and sisters, particularly the Muslims, on how the white man had used his pictures of a white Jesus to keep us blind from seeing the real Jesus...the Jesus that would set us free. If young African radicals, the future leaders, rejected Jesus on the basis of colour, then they would have no basis for unity and Africa would continue attracting killing machines to power, and the West would continue to exploit us. We desperately needed unity.

My words sounded good but rang hollow inside. Jesus was still meek and mild. How could He save Africa while turning the other cheek? How could a revolutionary like myself follow a leader who projected such a sense of frailty? As I looked back on His life before the age of thirty, it hit me that Jesus had worked with His father as a carpenter. Carpenters worked with heavy pieces of wood, lifting them, chopping them, carving them, finishing them. This was work for strong men. I reflected on the idea of Jesus being big, and brawny...two hundred pounds of solid man with muscles Mr. Universe would envy. I liked that. I could fight behind that man.

I listened carefully to the Easter story. Dr. Luke, in his Gospel, tells us that Jesus was in such agony before His crucifixion; His sweat became drops of blood. A condition, experts say, that makes skin very sensitive, yet Jesus was literally beaten half to death very shortly afterwards. An ordinary man would have died, but Jesus was still able to carry that heavy cross partway up a hill. I concluded He must have been a man of extraordinary physical strength.

I was getting into this. My outward picture of Jesus was turning out very well. I felt this was a man behind whom we could all unite. A man for all people. But something was still missing. Jesus' power and presence were not to be found in His physical body. To continue to worship Him in body was to deny the power of His resurrection. I had to move on from the worship of the flesh to the worship of the Spirit. I had to balance my Christianity. I could appreciate the physical, but it was His Spirit I was to worship.

Proverbs 16:16 says, "How much better it is to get wisdom than gold! And to get understanding is to be chosen above silver." I went before my God and asked Him to teach me about Jesus. I didn't want to know about the Jesus the world had fabricated, I wanted the real Jesus or nothing at all. I wanted to know Jesus like my father knew Him, and it was my father's teaching I sought the most. We wrote to each other regularly, and spoke on the phone. When his travels brought him through southern California, we would have long talks.

In one of his letters to me, dated July 6, 1985, Entebbe Airport, my father wrote the letter that revolutionized my walk with Jesus. It is a letter I have always wanted to share with my Christian brothers and sisters because what he wrote can bless and challenge all of us. Allow me here, to share some of that seven-and-a-half-page letter. Again, I want it to be of special blessing to fathers and their daughters, for the teaching and prayers of a righteous Dad availeth much.

My dear Viki,

Greetings in the name of the Lord Jesus!

I was very happy to hear you on the telephone, and there soon after, your letter arrived. I have been reading through it a number of times and oh, how I wish I could walk beside you and we could talk our hearts out. I am convinced that the Lord did a great work in your life. Reading your letter ushers me into a wonderful revelation of the mighty hand of God, which saves in spite of ourselves.

Keep it up and let Satan play NO part in what God has so graciously done for you. There is no other thing as important in this short span of our lives here on earth. To hold it firmly, build on it, sell it and draw all your needs in waiting upon the Lord, from it is the most exciting adventure. To live by the Spirit and not by the flesh. So allow me, Viki, you as one of the two dearest daughters, sweetest, loveliest and wonderful, a man can ever have in the world, allow me to share one point I have always wanted to put to you, and your very frank letter, for which I am most grateful, has been a great encouragement.

LIVE BY THE SPIRIT AND NOT BY THE FLESH.

GIVE JESUS A REAL CHANCE TO MAKE YOU A DONKEY FOR HIM TO RIDE!!!

For you and me who have known the Lord Jesus personally, we often suffer from insecurity and inability to enjoy our Faith in full! Why? Our inconsistency. Our blurred priorities and fear to lose out in the pressing economic, social and philosophical earthly balance. What will they say? How shall I...? Who am I when...?

I must fight for myself - becomes the temptation - and off we go.

Wait a bit - but there is God, we observe. Yes - the Lord - the Lord! Down on our knees we go - "Lord, do not fail me, I trust you - make me a winner!!!"

Our prayers are not answered because they give God no chance! His WILL is left out!

He is not unkind! If we pray according to HIS WILL, He will do as He promised.

HOW CAN I KNOW HIS WILL FROM MINE?

This is the gateway to a new life of satisfaction, because it is a life of service to GOD and HIS KINGDOM, which really matters.

To surrender oneself to this end is not an easy task, because of how we value ourselves, our talents, our education, our beauty and our worth - to the world around us!

It is the world around us that very often colours our priorities and the devil comes in clothed in good intentions and empty promises. Hence frustrations, and more hard work. To achieve that which can never be achieved, because the world does not offer satisfaction however successful one may be in fields, it offers loneliness.

So the world is an elusive customer and worldliness a bottomless and sad profession.

"The Cross before me and the world behind me," so goes a chorus - and "Even if my friends deny me, etc., I will not turn back. No turning back, etc.!!!"

Oh! Lord, I am writing to my dearest daughter - beloved and precious VIKI! Let Your Light penetrate these words with the power from You, GOD Almighty.

"Come to me all who are heavy laden - I will refresh you. Take my yoke - and learn of me, You will find rest!" Because - the thief does not come - but;

To steal - take away your faith and salvation, your joy, your peace and love of God.

To kill - bother your conscious with fear, frustration and temptation until you become immune to God's righteousness, forgiveness and His faithfulness. Compromise to double standards becomes inevitable failure and back to square one. Satan is happy, but not satisfied.

And to destroy - the thief only finds peace if he manages to destroy every evidence to us - until he has silenced us once and for all.

BUT GOD IN JESUS SAYS:-

"I CAME THAT THEY MAY HAVE LIFE AND HAVE IT ABUNDANTLY!!!!!"

HERE THEN LIES THE MISSING LINK TO REAL LIFE.

Viki, what is your greatest pre-occupation? Where have you invested? What are you selling? What profit are you looking for? Can God... be calling again?

"Fear not Peter - follow me and I will make you a fisher of men - you see - fish of the lake perish."

And Peter left everything and followed Jesus!

Viki, this is the message I want to go deep, to the very bottom of my heart - that for my last years here I may leave everything and follow Jesus my Lord. Everything I need for my passing days is in Him, if only my eyes can open to see!

"Oh ye nations, look to me and be saved!"

Hebrews 12:2.

Fix our eyes on Jesus. "I am the Door, anyone who enters by Me will be saved. (He) Viki will come in and go out AND WILL FIND THE PASTURE!" John 10:9.

This is where the Lord Jesus in the Power of the Holy Spirit pastures His FLOCK (SHEEP). Now He wants donkeys to take Him around as He gathers those lost to bring them back, those strayed to restore them, those crippled by sin to bind them up and those weak to give them strength! "AMEN."

"Here I am Lord - send me!"

Your mum is with me as we pray for you every day that God may reveal Himself more clearly and make His will your greatest ambition. Let Jesus be the greatest merchandise - sell Him in season and out of season. Invest in Him until your bank account is bursting and then issue eternal cheques to this sick world. "AMEN"

How I wish you get your Green Card soon, then you can give us a few months in Kampala towards our Greater Kampala Mission 85/86. I am fighting to find the money. If it works out - you can come as an advisor in Publicity, Press, and Communication...

I will send you a complete write up on Kampala Mission when it is ready.

Mum, Grandpa and Co. send greetings.

Yours ever -

Dad.

After I read that letter, the Lord answered my father's prayer. His Light penetrated my father's words with such power I was brought into deep conviction. I saw the compromises I had allowed in over the few years I had been a Christian. I found myself standing in the fire of love, tears streaming down my cheeks, much like my first encounter with God. This time I committed myself to Jesus, to be a donkey for Him. I immediately set my mind on wrapping up my business in America and returning to Africa to work alongside my father. I wanted to be near him, to be his apprentice, to learn from him how to be an authentic Christian. This was going to be the beginning of my great adventure.

I began to discover the dynamic to a successful relationship with Jesus— making Him a lifetime occupation. Making every day a new day to discover every possibility to invest in Him, to sell Him in and out of season. It was a costly proposition. Jesus sometimes asks us to lay down our lives for Him, and my father did just that eight months after he wrote that letter. I was to see him one last time that September.

Jesus became my revolutionary leader. In Him I found a good friend, a Shepherd, someone who understood my weaknesses and applauded my strengths. Someone I could take with me into every situation of life. I discovered that Jesus shining through me could meet all people wherever they were. Wherever I was, there I was to be "salt" to those whose lives had lost their flavour, and "light" to those whose bulbs had lost their light.

Jesus needed donkeys, people who would commit their lives to serve Him. As my father said in his letter, "..it is a life of service to God and His Kingdom which really matters." I stated earlier that my father showed me in a practical way how I was to relate to Father God, but in watching his life he gave me a first-hand view of Jesus in action. A view of Jesus I totally believed in, was very proud of, and wanted to be like.

As I read my Bible I was able to encounter the real Jesus. I saw a very special man who could rejoice with those who were rejoicing, grieve with those who were grieving. I found Him to be refreshingly practical, as shown by His first miracle when He gave the gift of new wine to some newly married friends, and uniquely sensitive, as shown when He refused to embarrass the woman caught in sexual sin.

I met the only man in all of history who was so completely colour blind He ate dinner with anyone who invited Him, Jew or Gentile, Christian or non-Christian, rich or poor. He was witty and fun-loving when He reclined with His disciples and friends after supper. He was a man who was very comfortable with His body, with His mind, with His emotions, a man of perfect character. He had a divine sense of His purpose and the discipline to fulfill it at any cost.

"For I have come down from heaven, not to do My own will, but the will of Him who sent Me." John 6:38. This was the statement that impressed me most about Jesus. Jesus had a will. He had the right to refuse to step anywhere near Calvary. He could have easily signed His own marching orders and split. But it was not His will that was important. He was in absolute surrender to the will of the Father, even if it meant experiencing the worst pain in human history—that of dying for the sins of all of humanity. He had total faith in the One who sent Him, and believed that the will of God was perfect. He was a man who worshiped God and was without fear. In short, He was the devil's worst nightmare.

That's what I wanted to be—the devil's worst nightmare. I wanted to pay him back for all the nonsense he'd put me through. Now I knew how—by becoming more like Jesus everyday, and living in absolute trust and obedience to His will. I took on the same purpose as Jesus—to destroy all the works of the devil.

Jesus was going to show me how. My human limitations were not important, everything hinged on my faith in Jesus. All He wanted from me was my heart in absolute surrender. He would work through me. He would cleanse me. He would purify me. He would fill me. Then He would hold me up as a light for a world covered in darkness. This meant discipline (not a dirty word in my dictionary), sacrifice, a lot of studying, a life bathed in prayer, and the memorization of 1 John 1:9, "If we confess our sins..."

Standing in the fire of love, I could no longer hold on to my prejudices, my hatreds, my petty jealousies and pride, my lust. I had to become a rational, truth-seeking believer and not one who was controlled by emotions. I could no longer sit back and watch the world parade its way to hell. I had to work fast and snatch as many fish out of the tide as I could, keeping my eyes on Jesus.

I wanted to accept His challenge to be a bold, vibrant, intelligent, transparent, exciting witness of His love and grace. I wanted my life to account for something. I wanted the world to be a little bit better just because I was in it, humbly carrying my Lord around as He healed the sick and fed the weak and hungry. I wanted to march up mountains with mighty warriors, calling to weary travellers to get up from under the captivity of this world, and be set free in Jesus' name. I wanted to stand beside my father at the mountain top, lifting Jesus up so He could draw all men to Himself.

Chapter 6

Call From The Center

My father was a man driven. J.I. Packer, in his book *Knowing God*, says that those who know God have great energy for God. My father confirmed that when he came through California on a whirlwind tour to raise support for his Uganda Peace Program. Saddened by the Church's response to the loss of human life in Uganda, he felt called by God to intensify his push towards uniting all the churches in Uganda to call for peace and reconciliation from one united platform.

In September 1985, he managed to squeeze into his itinerary a few days in Los Angeles to spend with us. The news from Uganda continued to be disappointing. Killings after killings. A six o'clock curfew made Kampala city into a ghost town by the evening.

My father outlined his vision from the pulpits of churches such as Rolling Hills Covenant, Bel Air Presbyterian, Lake Avenue Congregational. My personal favourites were the black churches with their exceptional music. He was a tall, elegant man of wonderful charisma, and I would sit in the pews of these racially diverse congregations captivated by his ability to capture their minds and excite them to support his ministry, both in prayer and financial support. He had a great burden for Uganda and people responded to his candid transparency.

His theme was always the same, reconciliation.

"The major challenge that faces Uganda today is that of healing the hearts and minds of a people who now know

no other way of settling their disputes than by the gun. We need to send a message to the people of Uganda that our future and the future of our children lies in our accepting our differences and uniting. The greatest responsibility rests with the Church of Uganda, for we have the Gospel of Jesus Christ."

He took me with him into his meetings. He briefed me in great detail on all God had accomplished so far. I remember wondering how one man could do all the things he was doing and still stay sane. It had come to the point that when asked about which countries he had been to, it was easier for him to say which ones he hadn't been to. Eighty percent of his letters to me were written on a plane, in an airport, or hotel room.

He challenged me to think through the issues facing Uganda and the Church. He wanted me to understand history correctly; the effects of colonialism in the African heart and psyche; the effects of the greed-driven, illogical boundaries that were erected around us by our colonial 'masters'—and were still a major contributing factor in our tribal differences. He wanted me to know the main division lines along which the Church in Africa was divided, separating the ecumenicals and evangelicals. He pointed out the major players: the All Africa Conference of Churches (AACC), and the Association of Evangelicals of Africa and Madagascar (AEAM); and those who were caught in the middle, who found the two camps complimentary to one another, a sort of 'third' way.

He listened prayerfully to my thoughts and ideas, my fears and struggles. I could trust him with my innermost feelings knowing he believed in me and always wanted the best for me...and he never gave up demanding excellence from me. He encouraged me to stand before groups of young people and share my faith. He was very proud when my calendar, *AFRICA THE WOMAN*, finally rolled off the press. He took some copies with him on his trips.

From Japan he wrote,

"I was seated on a train when we started a very hilarious situation with about 20 Japanese, they could not speak a word of English, but through all types of signs, we got on wonderfully. So, in showing family pictures I took out the 1980 group of 9, they brought theirs, then I produced your calendar! 'Oh be-a-utiful!' They wanted to take it."

In retrospect, I see how he was grooming me to carry on the vision. I remember a sense of urgency in his voice as he cautioned me to keep my eyes on Jesus, "Victoria, don't put me on a pedestal. I am only human; one day I'll be gone. Put your trust in God."

At the airport before he left California, he gave my brothers and me each a special bear hug before walking away. He turned and waved to us before disappearing into the boarding ramp. Little did I know, as I stood by the window crying silently, that that was the last time I was to see him alive. All I knew was that he was coming back in April the next year and I was to return with him to work on the Greater Kampala Mission.

Meanwhile, he had asked me to write a contribution to his reconciliation write-up, focusing on the problems of Uganda, specifically in the areas of:

1. Tribalism
2. Lust for power
3. Lust for things (ebintu)
4. Crime
5. False wishful thinking
6. Hate and Revenge
7. Lack of True Nationalism
        (people looking down on others)
8. A new heart and new direction.

When I returned to the apartment, I looked at the list and wondered if my father had gone totally mad. How could I write on all those subjects? I was smart, but not that smart.

He didn't stop there. He sent a letter outlining his desire to soften the hearts by the media.

"Say we start with

1. T.V. series, 15 minutes, 1x a month or more
2. Radio series, 15 minutes, 1x a month or more
3. Articles in newspapers
4. A Booklet of short messages
5. A Booklet of short testimonies
6. Posters and stickers
7. A newsletter every 6 months

What I want to ask you is, what do you think? Will the TV series be too expensive? The THEME would be - "'Come let us reason together,' says your God." Isaiah 1:18. A MINISTRY OF RECONCILIATION. When you get time jot down your thoughts and send them to me. I am drawing up my budget and would like to be more realistic. I wish you were here then you could direct them!!"

I began to have some serious doubts about working with my father. I would never be able to keep up with him. He seemed to operate in overdrive a little too much for my liking. I liked to rest. The word did not seem to exist in his vocabulary. He had more ideas in one year than most people have in a lifetime, and he had the persistence to see them through. Sometimes, though, the Lord intervened, as seen in one of his letters:

"I have been working on Uganda Reconciliation 24 hrs, but advice from interested parties has made it difficult to see the horizon. So, I am stepping on the brakes while I sort out who is saying what and the reasons motivating the good or bad sentiments. Meanwhile, I am doing a little carpentry, which is exciting. I am finishing a cupboard for Mummy. Two book shelves for my new office."

That didn't last long. Soon I received other letters;

"...I have sent a copy of my reconciliation program for

Uganda. I would treasure your input. Get some photo-stats and send me some feedback soon. It is gaining momentum both ways - for and against. Those in the bush - for, as this suggests coming out of the bush honourably. Against - are those to whom it is a threat, for whom it will not meet their wishful thinking in the 'status quo.' But when bigger bodies go for it, then we shall see some fun. It did cause some hours of anxiety, but that phase is gone as I have heard people of both sides speak to the future of Uganda - no hope, but killings after killings. I am pushing on in prayer and commitment to the Lord and to Uganda..."

"...I have not told you folks, AEE (African Evangelistic Enterprise - the organization he worked with) thought that the programme was so sensitive an issue that they decided to ask me to do it alone and not as a representative of AEE. Many people believe that this was the best they could have done. I am in full AEE programmes otherwise. So I am plodding carefully and with every prayer for direction and guidance.

The Lord has done wonders already. Now the Wide World Anglican Consultation Council is involved and have sent $5,000 support. The Pope has been told by the Archbishop of Canterbury, etc. The doors are opening slowly, what I see at the end as a base for the Programme is a world wide Church Assembly on Uganda's reconciliation..."

I knew I would never make it as his assistant when I saw him interviewed on a Christian talk show in Pittsburgh. After he had given a run-down of his impossibly busy schedule, he stated rather matter-of-factly;

"The other major programme I am working on is MECLA (Middle East Christian Leadership Assembly), which is now "CYPRUS '87" and will be held from 2nd to 12th November, 1987, at Larnaca.

We have ministered in Israel, in Egypt, in Bahrain, Jordan and Cyprus. We have already laid out groundwork in Syria and Turkey. We have come quietly from Africa with love to the household of God."

After that interview, he led a seven-person team on a historic, three-week visit to China at the invitation of Bishop Ting, China's influential Christian leader. This, alongside a tremendous ministry in North America, South America, Canada, Australia, New Zealand, and many countries in Europe, he still managed to write letters every step of the way, including one from Hong Kong and two from China.

He wrote,

"Tomorrow evening I start the home bound flight. You get a bit tired sometimes, especially when the mission is over, yet one has to wait for the flight going in the proper direction."

His efforts to bring peace to different parts of the world did not go unnoticed. He was awarded the Saint Augustine Cross from the Archbishop of Canterbury, and for his outstanding ministry of reconciliation, he was made a Companion of the Cross of Nails at Coventry Cathedral, an honour he valued greatly and which put him in an esteemed company of reconcilers recognized over the centuries for their work towards peace.

January 26, 1986, Yoweri Kaguta Museveni and his popular National Resistance Army stormed Kampala city and took control of the country after a five-year struggle in the bush. Ugandans were elated. The announcement was heard over Kampala radio and the people flew out of their houses. They spent the night in the streets singing and celebrating. Those who had pictures of Museveni held them high in the air. Three days later, Yoweri Kaguta Museveni was sworn in as President of Uganda. Peace had finally come to Uganda after sixteen-years of hell as one military regime after another sent the country into deep decline.

No one was more excited than my father. The day he and every Ugandan had prayed for had finally come, and at great human sacrifice. Many innocent Ugandans had laid down their lives for this moment, and to each one of them we are eternally grateful. To my father, this signaled his possible return to Uganda after so many years in exile. He felt that now more than ever Ugandans needed the message of reconciliation. We needed to put tribal hatreds aside if Uganda was to get a chance to be rehabilitated and reconstructed. He focused on Kampala and wasted no time scheduling a two-week trip into Uganda.

Sunday, March 16, I received the phone call. My father had been assassinated. Gunmen had tracked him down throughout that day until they stopped him at a makeshift roadblock and shot him in front of my mother and my grandfather (my mother's father), then made off with the car. My mother ran to find help. He died ten minutes after they got him to the hospital.

In shock, sitting in my apartment, 12,000 miles away from home, I knew I had to go back; I had to see the body for myself. I worried for my mother who had loved and shared her life with my father for thirty-four years. Now he was gone, shot before her very eyes. I was grateful to God that she had been spared.

The following days went by in a flurry of preparation: flight arrangements, packing. The nights were long and fitful. I was in a nightmare I could not wake up from. Wednesday evening, March 19, two of my brothers and I lifted off from Los Angeles International Airport heading for a homeland we hadn't seen in five years, and to the reality of our unfathomable loss.

Friday morning, March 21, the plane touched down at Entebbe Airport. The sister I had last seen at thirteen was now the tall, beautiful eighteen-year-old who fell into my arms sobbing. Weary from thirty hours of sleepless travel, I held her head to my shoulder and felt her pain. I looked up into the sad, brown eyes of my very tall younger brother, now twenty-two years old. He broke into a brave smile as we hugged and held onto each other.

Those were moments of sweet reunion filled with the deep pain of our sorrow. Words were not necessary. We had all loved him deeply; he had been a best friend to each one of us and his death shook us to the very foundations.

The twenty-three mile car ride from the airport to the city of Kampala was etched with the dreaded fear that every mile brought us closer to our grieving mother and the lifeless form of our beloved father. We were dismayed at the destruction of the buildings we passed, especially in Kampala city. As the car wound its way up Namirembe Hill to where my father lay in state in the home of the Right Reverend Misaeri Kauma, Bishop of Namirembe, not even the unrelenting potholes could keep our minds off our inner turmoil.

I sought refuge in the God who had given me the strength to endure it to this point, yes, even the wisdom to understand it. Matthew 5:9 says, "Blessed are the peacemakers, for they shall be called sons of God." The reconciler had been caught between two opposing forces and crushed.

In true African tradition, hundreds of people had gathered at the Bishop's home, not only to mourn with the family, but to mourn their own personal loss of a man who had been a good friend. As we were ushered into the small chapel, relatives and friends reached out to touch us, to comfort us. My eyes searched for my mother among the group sitting on mats around the raised coffin. I needed to hold her...to be held by her. I needed to know she was okay.

She was unaware of our arrival until I fell into her arms. She held my trembling body as I finally let it all out. I could hear her soft voice comforting me, "Daddy's in heaven. He's safe and rejoicing with the Lord." My mother, always strong, always dependent on the Lord. She looked drawn and tired, but she had to be strong for us. She took our hands and led us to the coffin. "Don't be afraid," she said. "He's a bit gray, but he looks peaceful." She lifted the cloth away from the upper part of the coffin and I looked at the still, ashen face of my father.

Later I was to spend twenty of the most intense minutes of my life, as I carefully smoothed make-up over his hardened features. It was just he and I. Everybody had been ushered out of the chapel. As the colour came back into his face, artificial though it was, I spoke to him and told him I didn't know which way was up anymore. I didn't know how to live in a world without him. My tears blurred my vision as I tried to comb his hair. I remembered the many times I had washed and conditioned it for him, the many times I had played beautician and given him facials. This was to be the last time.

An estimated seven thousand people showed up for the funeral the next day, some from as far as Australia, and California. Namirembe Cathedral overflowed with people out to its grounds, a true testimony to a man who had lived his life to glorify his Lord and Saviour. Over a hundred fully robed priests and clergy from every diocese in Uganda followed behind the casket which was held high by my five brothers and an uncle.

As I sat through the ceremony, numb with grief, I wondered why God had called my father home at the age of sixty three when he still had so much more to offer and he was still so full of energy and life. I wondered how life was to continue for me. As I watched the casket being lowered into the grave, I promised my father that if it had meant that much to him then his dream and his vision would go on. He was buried on the Cathedral grounds, an honour reserved only for those who had given exceptional service to God and the Church of Uganda. Our beautiful bulb that had shed so much love and light into our lives had been snuffed out.

Upon my return to America, I began to sink into the deepest, darkest valley of my life. The sense of loss overwhelmed me as I began to realize the finality of the death of a man who had been the center of my life. Life never had to make sense before just as long as my father was in it. I couldn't think of the fact that he wasn't in the world somewhere doing what he did best, inspiring people.

Now that my plans had been knocked out from under me, I had to stay in America for a while longer. How long? I didn't know anything any more...except that I felt so alone! My job welcomed me back and I delved into work thinking it would keep my mind busy, but things slowly got worse and my supervisor told me it was okay to take some time off. I kept telling her I was fine, but one day I was so physically and emotionally drained, I couldn't even force myself out of the house. I was crying uncontrollably. I know it was God's providence that put Ken into my life shortly before my father's death. We worked at the same company and had somehow fallen into the habit of having lunch together.

We had been reluctant to start a relationship knowing that I was leaving for Africa to work with my father, but we enjoyed each other's company and thought lunch would be harmless. After receiving the tragic news, Ken had been one of the first people I called. He was with me right from the beginning, sitting quietly with my brothers and me, and with those of our Ugandan friends who had come to offer their condolences. They, too, had all known my father and felt the loss.

It was Ken who took me to the airport the Wednesday evening we left for Africa. After the flight had been announced, he pulled me into his arms and gently wiped the tears from my cheeks. He whispered softly that he would be waiting when I came back. He called me several times during the two weeks I was in Africa, just to make sure I was okay.

Now I was back in California indefinitely and I was hurting. It was Ken who held my broken spirit together with his love. He was there no matter what time I needed him. He saw me in my rawest form and he hurt with me. The Lord knew the death of my father would have killed me had my grief not been tempered with my deepening love for Ken. There had been great concern for me among the many people at the wake and the funeral. Everyone knew how I had adored my father, and he left no doubts about how he felt about me.

Now I found myself groveling on the floor before the Lord. Up to that point I thought He had allowed me to understand my father's death, and spiritually I knew he was where he had always wanted to be, with his Jesus. He had certainly fought the good fight and had everything to look forward to in heaven. But it didn't change the fact that I was still on earth and floundering without him. News from Kenya was that my mother was falling apart. She had lost her will to live. With a roll of Brawny paper towels in my hands, I stayed on my knees beside my bed and wept to the Lord. There were moments I thought the pain would overtake me as I tried to come to terms with the fact that I would never see my father again. Something inside me had died with him.

Then I remembered a statement he had made to me the last day I saw him, "Victoria, the best gift I can give you as your father is to point you to Him who never disappoints. Trust Him in and out of season." I immediately fell on my stomach and asked the Lord to forgive me. I had put my father in the place that belonged to God. I had trusted my father with many of the decisions of my life, now the Lord was calling me to look to Him. He was the one who made me, who gave me life, who saved me, and who had a plan for my life. He had had a plan for my father and now his had come to completion and mine still had to go on.

I am one who sees myself in the situations I read about in the Bible. In Mark 8:23-25, is a story of a blind man. Jesus spit in his eyes and laid His hands upon him. The man looked up and he could see...he saw men, but they were like trees walking about. Jesus laid His hands on the man's eyes again, and this time he began to see everything clearly.

Up to that point I was looking at people as if they were trees, but now I began to see people as people who needed my love and my compassion. I could no longer live on my father's faith and on his visions. The time had come to claim my own path, directed by the Lord. It was time for me to define my terms and determine the principles I was going to live by. This was the start of my great adventure with the Lord. The call had come straight from the Center, and I responded, "Yes, Lord."

The way wouldn't always be without pain, but the Lord assured me He would be there every step of the way, every minute of every day. He had great plans for me, to give me hope and a future. My father had laid the foundations; I was to build upon them.

Rev. John Wilson addressing the
assembly at PACLA (Pan African
Christian Leadership Assembly),
Nairobi, Kenya, December 1976.

Commissioning service and
presentation of St. Andrew's Cross.
(l-r:) The Rt. Rev. Festo Kivengere,
the Archbishop of Canturbury, the
Rt. Rev. Misaeri Kauma, the Rev.
John E. H. Wilson.

John Wilson with his friend
Michael Cassidy, founder of
African Evangelistic Enterprise.

(photos courtesy of African Enterprise.)

John Wilson and his Mary.

On the beach at Carmel, California, 1980.

Pasadena, California, 1975.

Nairobi, Kenya, 1985.

A Wilson family portrait, 1972, Kampala, Uganda.

(l-r, back row:) Edward, Moses, Albert, Victoria, Philip.

(l-r, front row:) Dad, Betty, Mum, Daniel.

Dad and his daughter Victoria, Jinja, Uganda, 1958. There was a special bond between father and daughter from the very beginning.

Victoria, by now a confirmed tomboy. Family vacation, Mombasa, Kenya, 1970.

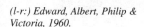

(l-r:) Edward, Albert, Philip & Victoria, 1960.

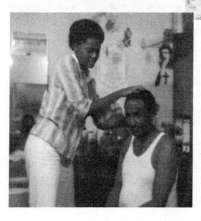

Victoria playing beautician. Nairobi, Kenya, 1981.

Dad with his beloved mother, Eseza Nakawungu, Namawojolo, Uganda, 1981.

Dad bringing his father back to Kenya for medical treatment, 1981.

Edward Wilson, Sr. with his son John Wilson, in better days, Uganda, 1979.

Family picture, Christmas 1979, Pasadena, California. (l-r:) Mummy, Betty, Daniel, Moses, Victoria, Philip, Albert, Edward, Daddy.

*PACLA, 1976. (l-r:) The Rt. Rev. Bishop Festo Kivengere, his wife Mera,
Rev. John Wilson, Dr. Billy Graham, Rev. Gottfried Osei-Mensah.*

*John Wilson giving a good word for Jesus to a willing audience in
Karamoja, Uganda, 1981.*

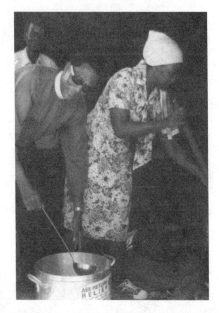

My father loved children. With refugee child in Karamoja, 1980.

Mum & Dad in kitchen, Soroti Primary School, 1981.

Man in refugee camp, He died ten minutes after this picture was taken. Soroti, 1980.

John Wilson in his element-teaching children about Jesus. Karamoja refugee camp, 1981.

*The realities of
Uganda. Children in
Karamoja.*

*Victoria holding the
hand of a dying child.
Karamoja, 1980.*

*Typical roadblock along
Uganda's roads. 1980.*

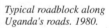

John Wilson greeting a Chinese girl at the highest point of the Great Wall. Beijing, China, October 1985.

Graduation from USC. (l-r:) Victoria, Edward, Moses, Albert, Dad. 1980.

John Wilson's funeral. The casket is carried by his sons. Namirembe Cathedral, 1986.

John Wilson and Victoria. My friend, Cheryl Davis Sharp, took these pictures, little knowing it was the last time I would see my father. Pasadena, California, September 1985.

Ken and Victoria's wedding. (l-r:) Rt. Rev. Misaeri Kauma, Albert, Ken's sister Beth, her friend Colin, Mum, Moses, Victoria, Ken, Ken's dad Thomas Darragh, his mum Josephine, Daniel, Betty, Enoch Kauma. October 1988.

Bishop Kauma performing the wedding.

Moses Wilson's marriage to Denni. (l-r:) Albert, Daniel, Betty, Denni, Moses, Mum, Edward, Victoria, Philip. November 1993.

Victoria & Jordan,
Pasadena, California, 1991.

Ken & Jordan, December 1990.

Victoria & Jordan writing a screenplay,
January 1990.

Jordan, Ken & Victoria,
Pasadena, California,
1991.

The boys club, December
1990. (back row, l-r:)
Moses, Albert (front l-r)
Daniel, Ken & Jordan.

*John Wilson
conducting a
service,
San Marino,
California, 1980.*

Dad playing
Sorry! *with Betty.
California, 1975.*

*Visiting with Jerry &
Bunny Fish. (l-r:) Jerry,
Bunny, Ken, Victoria,
Jordan, Moses, Grace,
Albert. Sacramento,
California, 1991.*

Chapter 7

Understanding God's Forgiveness

To be in love with God means to be in love with the Bible and in love with prayer, because those two things connect you personally with your heavenly Father in a very unique way.

One is His love letter to you, the other is His love song. During those intense months of grief after my father's death, I developed a very private, very special life of prayer. I was myself with God. I could let it all out while tucked safely away under His wings. Those were definitely days when He carried me. There is a saying that God calls upon those who have felt pain. Pain is His blowtorch, and although it is only one of many instruments in The King's Forge, it happens to be the hottest. In His forge, God breaks us, melts us, cleans us, purifies us, molds us, fills us, then uses us. I had reached the blowtorch and was being melted to be a vessel for His service.

When I first came into The Forge in 1982, I was dirty. Not as dirty, thank God, as I was diligently seeking to become, but dirty nonetheless. I had used and abused my vase emotionally and physically. I needed major forgiveness. I needed major cleaning. By faith I had opened the door into The Forge and stepped into fresh air, into green pastures. It was great. It was wonderful. All I had to do was check in with my Saviour and Guide, Jesus Christ, and have Him help me identify my path as set by God. Together we would embark on a journey to find out all my possibilities. I was anxious to find my path and start running.

In The Forge, I read the Bible with the same passion I had displayed when seeking to destroy it. As I looked at myself in the light of Jesus, I knew I needed major reconstruction (which I found out was to continue throughout my life!). The decision to accept Christ as the Lord of my life meant I was to remain under the scrutiny and protection of The King, being recalled at any time a tune-up was deemed necessary, going from one instrument of the Lord to another in a process called pruning and growing. I figured that all would be okay as long as I stayed clear of the blowtorch.

Then all around me I began to see Christians who had chosen to stay clear of the blowtorch, and had opted for the comfort over pain route, imprisoned by security. They were littered around the outskirts of The Forge. At first they seemed to have it all together, then as I got to know them they became boring and predictable. Their attention was wrapped up in things too petty for words. Their Christianity was just a crutch; there was no "first love" encounter with Jesus. Plenty of God-words, but no heart. None of their discussions of the Bible ever seemed to translate into practical application.

Then I began to smell them. They had a repulsively fake aroma around them. Underneath the squeaky-clean topcoats, the designer deodorants and perfumes, were hidden all kinds of little demons that needed the blowtorch (maximum level) to clean them out. Guilt had them racked up so badly they were seeing therapists. Even the therapists had therapists. It was actually 'in vogue' to be seeing someone for something or other. Dysfunction was the societal norm. The blind were leading the blind, and they were falling into all sorts of ditches. They were collectively suffering from a disease called 'low pain threshold,' common symptom— the demon of selfishness. Number one killer of spiritual fire and vitality, whose appetite knows no end. Nothing a trip to the side streets of Calcutta wouldn't cure. Even a small thing like helping someone across the street would begin to melt it down.

Then I noticed their cycle. Dr. Charles Swindoll describes it best in his book, *Living Above The Level Of Mediocrity*; they were either "...grubbing for worms or scratching for bugs like a pen full of chickens..." They were comfortable, they were pain free, risk-free, responsibility-free, but they were reduced to lives whose main goal was to snag worms and bugs. Fishers of men, they were not. They had managed to alienate the single most dynamic aspect of their forge experience—Jesus, and were now no better off than the people on the outside who longed to find the door out of the darkness but couldn't seem to find the key. And naturally, sadly, there weren't enough Christians willing to get out into the trenches and give them a helping hand.

Didn't the chickens realize how incredibly privileged they were to even be in The Forge? Didn't they care that they were hand-picked by Jesus to be in there? How could they take the most incredible miracle in the world, salvation, and avoid the reason for it—a personal relationship with Jesus here on earth as well as for eternity? My Jesus was not on the cross; He was with me, walking on terra firma. Theirs was still on the cross, still dead. To them the idea of a risen Saviour was still a mystery, and their concept of a spiritual world was rather ambiguous.

After some attempts to get that point across to those I had encounters with, I concluded they liked the darkness, for they were certainly living dangerously close to it, no matter how much I warned them of it. I could see now why the Lord would opt for spitting them out rather than keeping them around; they were too much of a pain to have around. If they weren't thirsty, then they had to make room for those who were.

During my 'honeymoon' in The Forge, I made the decision to begin my journey towards the Center; nearer to the heart of God. That's where I belonged, with Abraham and Moses, and Sarah and Naomi, you know, the great ones. I wanted to be refined by fire. I wanted to be transparent like the gold in heaven. I wanted to have uncommon obedience like Daniel, and Joseph, and John.

I wanted to have uncommon love like David and Solomon.

I wanted Jesus to tell me, "Well done, my good and faithful servant."

I wanted to be an eagle. I had been given wings to fly. Jesus had signed my flight certificate. I was anxious to get on with my mission. I felt reckless for Christ. What did I have in common with chickens in a crowded pen, who were too busy grubbing for worms to make time for Jesus? I wanted to pick fruit from any tree I wanted. I was a Wilson—bred for the pursuit of perfection and excellence. In my favourite movie, *Yentl*, our heroine makes the point that, "Sometimes where danger lies, there the sweetest of pleasures are found." So, I figured, spiritual discipline would beget spiritual excellence. I would learn to fly and then soar happily beside Jesus forever, enjoying this fruit and that fruit. I soon learned, however, that it was one thing to be in love with God, and another to be obedient.

Those early years in The Forge were...interesting. I was absolutely, unashamedly, unequivocally born again, but I was also decidedly young and nubile. It was one thing to discipline the body with good eating habits and regular exercise; it was another to discipline that body to stay out of bed with other equally raging bags of hormones, especially when it had been programmed to jump in.

I learned my first valuable lesson when I shared my mission with the chickens. ***Never tell chickens your plans.*** They will see to it that they DESTROY them, even if it means sending their finest roosters after you. If you must tell them, wait until you are far above their reach. It felt like I had walked into a minefield. "How could anything that feels so good be bad?" they crooned in my ears. I memorized verses that told me that if I resisted the devil, he would flee from me, but I must not have resisted hard enough or the devil didn't know how to flee, because my body kept putting me right in the middle of those explosives. Each detonated bomb set me back severely in my walk.

I began to wonder if I was destined to live a life of moral failure. How could the Lord ever get me clean enough to fill if I kept getting dirty? I thought once you were in The Forge you were not supposed to struggle with things like sex. I thought you weren't supposed to still enjoy reefer. How come when my alcoholic, chain-smoking father came to the Lord at the age of thirty-three, he was instantly delivered from his drinking and smoking? Why was this deliverance business selective? I wanted instant deliverance, too. I didn't want to struggle with sin.

My inability to rein in my hormones was creating rifts in my relationship with God. It kept me dangerously low to the ground. I'd see Jesus standing quietly to the side, and out of embarrassment I'd pull an Adam-and-Eve number. As I looked around at my compadres I found out they were struggling with the same explosives. Sometimes we stepped on the same explosive, and were then caught up in a web of guilt and shame as we struggled to get up and back on the road. Obedience (which begets righteousness) was proving to be a worthy instrument in its own right, but I didn't want to get caught up in the cycle of constantly falling and repenting, falling and repenting. Eventually the falling would overtake the repenting and I would be stuck in the chicken pen. I wanted the repenting to overtake the falling. I wanted the power and the freedom of God's forgiveness. I wanted to raise my Jesus high above the world, so He could draw His children to Himself.

Meanwhile, I certainly wasn't being a very good example. I looked at the lives of those ahead of me. How did they manage to overcome the beast within? How did they turn off the society that dripped with sensuality? How did they manage to stop the sewage from leaking into their hearts and mind? Then I looked all around me at those who were falling and being sucked back into the pen. That prospect was too horrifying to even contemplate. I had to get out and stay out. If I didn't want the fruits of sin, then it behooved me to stay out of the devil's orchard. I sent out the S.O.S. Only Jesus could get me out and keep me out.

It was in one of Corrie ten Boom's books that I found a rock to stand on. She gave the analogy of a church bell. When the devil leaves our lives, he takes the bell cord and gives it one last, good pull. The poor bell swings back and forth, back and forth with tremendous speed. But then something happens—the bell starts to slow down, and eventually it comes to a stop.

Maybe I wasn't one of those fortunate enough to have the devil flee without pulling my strings, but I could bring the desires of my flesh under the control of the Holy Spirit, one step at a time. I had to deprogram my body, and each step I took towards the Center was a step in the right direction. I had to realize that when I sincerely asked for forgiveness, I was instantly forgiven. I had to block out the devil's attempts to keep my mind wracked with guilt. I had to accept that forgiveness, shed the heavy cloak of shame and keep moving forward. For when Jesus set me free, He set me free indeed.

I became extremely wary of anything (friends, habits, unrepentance, non-acceptance of God's forgiveness, the devil, gravity, whatever) which threatened to pull me down. One would expect that my war was mainly with the world, but it was the chickens in the pen that were notorious for pecking people back into their fold. They wanted everybody to be mediocre and were very concerned with numbers at their stale Wimpy Christianity Church. Their motto was, 'Rope 'em back, by any means necessary. We need their money.' This was the way they had chosen to use their Godgiven passion.

I was not interested in 'wimpy' anything, and their cheap pleasures were robbing me of my joy. But...they were dangling some kinda apples before me, fine, young specimens who were ready, willing and able. It was all I could do to keep from taking a bite....

I had to make a choice, otherwise my indecision was going to determine my future. And quite frankly, I had no fondness for the creepy crawly things I would meet in the middle of those apples. I decided to drop my old friends who were pulling me down.

When that first sharp pang of loneliness struck, I felt like Peter in Matthew 14:30 & 31, "But seeing the wind, he became afraid, and beginning to sink, he cried out, saying, 'Lord, save me!' And immediately Jesus stretched out His hand and took hold of him, and said to him, 'Oh you of little faith, why did you doubt?'"

The first thing that hit me when I was finally able to look Jesus' in the eyes again was love. Blinding love. There was not even a hint of condemnation for all the sin I had brought with me into The Forge. In His eyes I did not see disappointment, just grace. When I made the choice to stand in the fire of that love, I chose to walk in Truth, for in His presence there was no darkness, just Light. I couldn't hide anymore. "Where can I go from Thy Spirit? Or where can I flee from Thy presence?" Psalm 139:7. I had to embrace reality with truth and grace...and hand the reigns of my life to Jesus.

"And from everyone who has been given much shall much be required; and to whom they entrusted much, of him they will ask all the more." Luke 12:48.

I had an unfair advantage over the friends I was leaving in the chicken pen; I had been taught to despise mediocrity within myself. Critical thinking and honesty were heavily enforced in our home. My siblings and I had learned very early in life that lying to my father was a fruitless exercise. He never even had to punish us, he just had to look into our eyes and shake his head. Then he would say, "Okay, now tell me the truth." The forgiveness was a given, we just had to tell him the truth.

There were times when I chose to withhold the truth. I didn't lie, I just wouldn't tell my father anything. That was allowed in certain situations. I was exercising my right to privacy. He went merrily along his way, leaving me feeling detached and miserable. He never disconnected himself from me, I disconnected myself. My guilt and pride stopped me from reaching out, but he knew, and I knew that eventually I would humble myself and run back into his arms. And they would always be open because his love for me was so wonderful.

Our favourite quote on disobedience was: "You only drown when you stay in the water." My father knew he had a strong-willed child, and he gave me the time and space necessary for the waves to knock me around a little and break that stubborn streak. It's that same stubborn streak that kept stalling my progress with the Lord, and sometimes His methods weren't so gentle because I took so long to turn around and come back to Him. Certainly, any way He chose to break me was not likely to be painless; and break me He had to because He was a holy God and He could not fellowship with sin, so He had to cleanse me of it before I could enter into more than a superficial relationship with Him.

> *"When I kept silent about my sin, my body wasted away through my groaning all day long. For day and night Thy hand was heavy upon me; my vitality was drained away as with the fever heat of summer." Psalm 32:3*

> *"'Come now, and let us reason together,' says the Lord, 'Though your sins are as scarlet, They will be white as snow; Though they are red like crimson, they will be like wool.'" Isaiah 1:18*

> *"I acknowledged my sin to Thee, and my iniquity I did not hide; I said, 'I will confess my transgressions to the LORD'; and Thou didst forgive the guilt of my sin." Psalm 32:5*

My inability to live without God's love eventually brought me to my knees, and even as I was confessing my sins, His forgiveness was already freeing me from guilt just as He had promised. In Jesus' hands, that stubborn streak became courage, because His promises to me were true. His perfect love did cast out my fear, His strength was sufficient for my weakness. Eventually, life began to turn right side up again and Jesus and I pressed happily on toward the goal for the prize of my upward call of God in Christ Jesus. The repenting overtook the sinning. We had managed to silence the bell (I thought).

I started to feel a little cocky, like I had this forgiveness thing down. But no one was more surprised than I when I found myself in an old boyfriend's house groveling on the bathroom floor, weeping my eyes out. How had I let him slip in? I had let my guard down for just one minute. In my eagerness to lead the young man to the Lord, I had allowed him to put a glass of wine into my hand. Then after some struggle with my conscience, I had taken the joint from his fingers. I rationalized, "Just one hit won't hurt." One thing had led to another. I had done the very thing I disdained in the chickens—I had compromised my commitment to Jesus, again. Once, twice, three times in one regrettable evening. Peter could not have felt worse on his fateful evening when he denied his Lord. I knew Jesus loved me, but I felt so weak, so stupid...so used...so dirty.

"If we confess our sins, He is faithful and righteous to forgive us our sins and to cleanse us from all unrighteousness." 1 John 1:9.

I'd blown it, but this time Jesus was not very far. I hadn't left Him outside in the cold, I had taken Him into my situation. The wine and pot had obscured Him for a moment, but now I turned to Him immediately and put out my hand. I was not going to stay in the water a minute longer. I was not going to let the devil convince me I was destined to fail, or that I needed to do something to earn it. I was going to believe by faith that upon my confession Jesus had forgiven me and cleansed me from my unrighteousness.

Jesus wrapped his fingers around my hand and pulled me up. As I stepped out of the house I tried to shut the memory behind me. I would never step in that house again. Little did I know as I walked away that Jesus was going to use that situation to reveal Himself to me in a new and wonderful way.

One thing I did know was that I was humbled. I knew someone who would sympathize with me—Paul. He had lamented on how he could never do the good he wished to do, and always ended up doing the very evil he did not want to do. Walking quietly beside Jesus, I took some time to think through some of the shaky doctrine that I had acquired from the Church. I thought about the thorn in Paul's side in 2 Corinthians 12:7, "...a messenger of Satan to buffet me—to keep me from exalting myself."

"Do you think it was a sickness?"

Jesus' question had startled me and I quickly glanced around. It had been so clear, almost audible. Where had it come from? Then it hit me that I had entered into a part of The Forge that was literally filled with the presence of Jesus. True humility had allowed Jesus to completely clear the air waves. I could now tune in clearly for instruction and direction. Jesus' presence became so real I could actually talk with Him just as I would any friend.

Did I think the thorn in Paul's flesh was a sickness? The more I thought about those sickness theories, the more they sounded like a cover up. I had had malaria many times; one bout had even hospitalized me for a week, but I would not have necessary called it a messenger from Satan; it had not solicited my humility, it had only elicited sympathy and great care from my mother, regular doses of Nivaquin...then I got better. What Paul was talking about sounded more like a vice to me.

Those decent, very proper pastors weren't saying it from their pulpits, but Paul was a human being, a single man; he had desires, he had thoughts; he wasn't simply struggling with malaria. What was so shameful about having malaria that he couldn't name it? He wrote about everything else for the sake of the Gospel. (Though I'd quite understand if he had chronic hemorrhoids, or something like that). Anyway, what was it he kept doing that he didn't want to do? Whatever it was, he hadn't deemed it edifying to expose in his letters, except to say that it kept him humble. And if I knew anything about Satan, he wouldn't simply send Paul a messenger of sickness, he would send him a messenger of sin...a sin specifically designed for Paul's soft spots, to knock him out. That was his game plan for me. The devil had sent his messenger of sin, custom designed for me, meaning it for evil, but thank God, Jesus had turned it into good. In fact He was now quite proud of me, which blew my mind again. He applauded my quick turn around. Now that was a high! I was hooked. Jesus was proud of me, who else's opinion did I need beyond that? We were going to work on shortening those delays even more.

I was beginning to slowly understand God's forgiveness. He had paid a tremendous price to be able to offer me a clear passage around, over, under, (through, if I insisted) those explosives. I needed Him. I couldn't do it alone. But I didn't have to do anything to deserve it - the price had already been paid—my sins were nailed through to the bone, on The Cross by Grace. I just had to come to my senses (hopefully sooner than later), ask God for His forgiveness and accept it by FAITH. Then I had to put my wings in gear and keep moving forward in sheer gratitude for such love, so undeserved, so divine.

I had been given much. Not one talent, not two; I seemed to have been given five. Thus I was required to bring back, at the very least, ten. I had been blessed, through my father, with a message the world needed to hear. I knew that God loved me. I knew He adored me. He knew that I loved Him and adored Him. Many of those coming up behind me were struggling to understand and experience that kind of love with Father God. They didn't understand the Father who loved them in spite of themselves, who did not punish them for the truth, but rather rewarded it. A Father who longed to take them under His wings and love them back to health. A Father who was behind them no matter what, who wanted only excellent things for them, and who would never let them down. Again, I heard the voice.

"The one who knows must teach the others."

How was I going to teach that to my friends in the pen? How could I get that message to all those around The Forge that were trapped behind bars: mental, physical and spiritual? Defeated.

How could I convince my therapy seekers and their therapists that what they were looking for was really God's love. It was God's forgiveness they were so desperately in need of understanding and accepting. So many people were needlessly trapped in mental institutions simply because they did not understand God's forgiveness. Yet it was there for them simply for the asking! God really and truly loved them with a wonderful love and had a dynamic plan for their lives—a plan to free them from a chicken-pecked life to an eagle's triumphant soar.

"The best teaching is by example."

Oh, boy, that hadn't been my forte to date. But now with my hand locked back securely in Jesus' hand, and my feet on solid ground again, I made a vow to do better. Yesterday was a cancelled check. Tomorrow was just a promissory note. I had today, cash on the barrel. A new day to set a better example and live a practical, intelligent, balanced Christianity. Yes, Lord, send me. I will teach them about You and show them how wonderful loving You is.

My face broke out into a smile. My spirit rose to the heavens with song. I broke forth in dance as I worshiped my Father in Heaven.

"Thou has enclosed me behind and before, and laid Thy hand upon me. Such knowledge is too wonderful for me; it is too high, I cannot attain to it." Psalm 139:5 & 6.

Chapter 8

The Missionary Enterprise

I'm sitting behind my desk looking at a piece of paper. On it are three solitary words; JAIL. HOSPITAL. CEMETERY. Jesus is sitting beside the desk facing me. I look up and wait for Him to speak. He isn't in a hurry. That's one thing I've come to accept...Jesus is never rushed. I study the words again. JAIL. HOSPITAL. CEMETERY. So soon after my father's death, I can't miss the implications. He looks at me and squints His eyes in that way that tells me He's about to ask a very serious commitment from me. I keep my eyes focused on His, afraid that if I look away I'll buckle and faint.

I'm in the forge that has appropriately been called by those who have gone before me, "Counting-the-Cost-Station." I'm encouraged by their example and listen as Jesus begins to talk:

> **"The choice you have made is a very serious one. The men and women you will find in this forge are those who have chosen to serve me even if it takes them to jail, or to the hospital, or even to the cemetery. They have all weighed the consequences, counted the cost, proven their faith, and have progressed on into the battle. Those whom you wish to serve with are on the frontlines. They have all answered the question that I must pose before you now. Victoria, are you willing to die for me?"**

How can He ask me that? Doesn't He know? Am I not here, after all? Jesus smiles at me as He continues to speak.

"Yes. You're here. And, as your father would say, 'First class decision'. You have shown your mettle. However, when I say 'die', I don't just mean physical death. Those on the frontlines have already died, and are dying daily, to their hatreds, their selfishness, their lust, their indifference, their hypocrisy, their pride. They have chosen to seek first the Kingdom of God and its righteousness in love from a pure heart, a good conscience, and a sincere faith."

Now, He had me. Physical death was a much easier choice for me than to die to myself. I still had visions of fame and fortune. I still had unresolved racial hatred. I could still hear the call of the wild. I still thought evil thoughts. I still had pride in my heart. I had developed contempt for the chickens. I was not always gracious. I was not necessarily compassionate. I hated America; too much of the church was pathetically trapped in the pen. I wanted to go home. I wanted to fight in Africa where Spirit-filled eagles soared, slaying flea-bitten demons in their paths. I still had too many wants. I still wanted too much control. Was I willing to give up the "I" plan? All of it?

"That is the battle, and it is located in your mind, which is housed by your body. You lose it in the mind and you've lost it."

Yes. And we both knew what a headache my mind and body could be. They were hard to reel in. The battle may very well not be against flesh and blood, but my blood still had potential rage as it coursed through my body.

"What happens with the chickens, they allow their emotions and feelings to dictate their choices. They are still only capable of operating in the flesh, rather than in the spirit. In this forge the Holy Spirit teaches and empowers you to have control over your emotions and feelings by engaging your mind. He will teach you practical, moral obedience."

I stare back at Jesus. What choice do I have, considering who my father was? I know too much. I don't have the luxury of mediocrity. My father always said that those who didn't have the taste for excellence should not sit at the table of opportunity. Jesus went to great lengths to ensure me a place at that table, and I'm not going to let Him down. I also have nothing to hide, even if I could. He knows my weaknesses, He knows my faults, yet He still considers me worthy material for His army and wants me in it, possibly even on the frontlines one day, in my father's place. Jesus' face softens.

> *"So... you want uncommon love and uncommon obedience? That is what you have requested of God?"*

I nod cautiously. It's a big order, given my downfalls.

> *"Are you sure you have the stuff of a David? Or the love of a Solomon, or the tenacity of a Paul? Or the conviction of a John Wilson?"*

No. I don't have it, but I am convinced that Jesus has it and He can work through me. I just have the want to and a little bit of courage. I've already experienced my worst nightmare, and Jesus didn't fail me. With Him, I have nothing to lose and everything to gain. I just pray that it's not too painful. I've never been too crazy about pain. Jesus can't help the smile that creeps onto His face. He shakes His head as He presents me with a set of fatigues, boots and all.

> *"It will often be lonely as far as people go, but you will always have me. How about that for a bargain?"*

I'll take it. I admire myself in my new duds. I've made it. I'm in soldier gear, and it feels fantastic. I feel powerful; Jesus has a special mission for me. Watch out, devil, here comes Sister Soldier. I'm glad I've been working out at the gym. It helps to look and feel the part.

> *"I'm glad, too. Stamina makes our journey that much easier. Too many soldiers have a willing heart and a willing mind, but they are hopelessly out of shape, so we can't ask them to*

> **jump too high...they might get a heart attack.**
> **Continue to encourage them as you go along."**

I resolve to intensify my workouts, my Bible reading, my prayer life, and to eat healthier. Jesus gets up, stretches and motions me outside. Elated, awe-struck, and in great anticipation, I follow Him. I pull myself up and push my shoulders back as I try to imitate His super-confident stride. I can't help singing when the first ray of beautiful sunshine hits me. I sing to heaven, "Oh Lord, my God, when I in awesome wonder, consider all the works Thy hands have made...How great Thou art!"

> **"You were made exactly to specification for**
> **this job. Only you can do it. I am glad you**
> **accepted the call because otherwise all your**
> **gifts would be wasted, like so many others."**

From the sad expression that falls fleetingly on His face, I get the feeling Jesus grieves deeply for all the lost souls that never get to sing their songs. I don't like that look on Jesus' face any more than I liked it on my father's. I'll go, Jesus, send me. I'll bring them back for You. Whatever it takes, just tell me what to do and I'll go...please, just don't look so sad.

We pass a sign that reads Soldier Training Camp. On the other side of the street, pointing the opposite direction there's a sign that reads Chicken Pen. Jesus anticipates my puzzled, though not necessarily ignorant, expression.

> **"Nowhere in this program are you ever forced**
> **to do anything. The choices are put out for you**
> **to consider, but you make the final decision.**
> **You can drop out any time. To succeed, you**
> **must become a focused and critical thinker."**

Just then a shout comes in from the chicken pen. A voice I recognize accuses me of being self-righteous and proud. I jump quickly, and in my anger stomp it out. How dare that little, insignificant, dysfunctional twit pull that stunt on me? Jesus stops to give me a moment to reflect on it. I try to avoid His gaze. A rift has come inbetween us. Man! What happened? How did I let her get to me like that? Just when things were going so well. I want to leave her on the floor, so I try to walk forward hoping Jesus will drop it. I look back and Jesus is kneeling beside the girl, wiping her tears. I panic. I have to walk back in the direction of the chicken pen!

I sit down. I look at the road ahead of me, but it's dark. Pitch black. I look back and look at Jesus. I notice, for the first time, the pained look on His face. He seems to be telling the young woman, "The insults of those who insult you have fallen on me." Romans 15:3b. I didn't hurt that young woman half as much as I hurt Jesus. He looks at me and silently reminds me of the verses before that. Romans 15:1,2 & 3a. "We who are strong ought to bear with the failings of the weak and not please ourselves. Each of us should please his neighbour for his good, to build him up. For even Christ did not please Himself...."

This dying to self business begins at point A. It doesn't even give one a chance to enjoy himself. As I sit there on the bench, I am aware that there is no advancement without Jesus. I am also painfully aware that there is no Jesus without humility and repentance. I strike up a conversation with another wounded soldier, benched by moral disobedience. I try to make him see my side. The woman's own self-righteousness was the root of the problem. If she'd kept her mouth shut all this would not have happened. The soldier and I look at each other, we both know we aren't the judges in each other's cases. The Judge has obviously sided with my opponent.

The soldier looks tentatively over at Jesus, and as if a bolt of courage hits him, he jumps to his feet. He has decided to humble himself before Jesus and repent of his sins. He runs over and falls into Jesus' open arms. A sharp pang of jealousy sweeps over me. I want that, but my stupid pride is standing in the way. I can't even bring myself to like that silly girl. Jesus' voice rings softly in my ears, "True soldiers are those who control their feelings, their feelings don't control them. Let your mind take over. Let me love her through you."

My mind knows what to do, but I can't get my heart, or my soul, to connect. I muster up some energy and stand up, but my feet refuse to move. "My eyes are ever on the Lord, for only He will release my feet from the snare." Psalm 25:15. The Lord. The Lord. I have to look at Jesus. I'm ashamed. I used unnecessary anger and force in dealing with the girl, knowing full well I was older and stronger. I should have been wiser.

I need to engage the mind. I know the longer I delay the worse I will feel, so I turn and look at Jesus. My feet take on wings. He opens up His arms and takes me back. Then He shows me my sister. I run towards her, take her in my arms and cry with her. She stops crying and I try to help her up, but she doesn't respond. I start to get a little impatient with her, but Jesus gently takes my hand and leads me on. "She's not ready," He says, "give her time." We leave her. I feel free again. Not ecstatic. The turn around was too long. But...I have today, and I have Jesus to help me work on my attitude. Tomorrow will be better. Jesus nods and smiles.

"The Lord is my Shepherd, I shall not want. He makes me lie down in green pastures; He leads me beside quiet waters. He restores my soul; He guides me in the paths of righteousness for His name's sake." Psalm 23:1-3.

Times of solitude. Times to sit at Jesus' feet, listening to Him, learning from Him. Times to share my fears and my desires with Him, and to express my love for Him. These are the times I live for. Times to learn about my God. Quite often they are hard, but that's what gets my adrenaline pumping—when I accomplish a task He has given me.

I prepare myself now. I know I'm in for a lesson. I sit quietly, patiently, waiting for Jesus. I want to be as cooperative as possible, because I have found out that the quicker I learn the lesson the quicker we move onto bigger challenges. I am young, I still have pride, I still make a lot of stupid mistakes, but I'm not afraid to face the truth. My father's lifestyle of openness and trust instilled in me the ability to be very open and honest about my feelings.

On the plane from Los Angeles, after I bid my father goodbye for the last time, he wrote an eight page letter which he concluded by saying;

"...I shall write as we go on so that we may enjoy the gift of openness and love which God has given us.

Your loving Dad."

It is easier to live that way. It is the only way to live with Jesus, who now speaks slowly and deliberately.

"You have been called. You have been given the strength and the courage...and the desire to continue the vision. But we have a long way to go before you have the maturity. You must get a hold of that temper."

How long have I been praying for gentleness? How long have I asked for graciousness? Wasn't it You who promised that if I asked for something I would get it? Why am I not gracious yet? I study the cover of my Bible. I remember a conversation I had with my father several years before. I had just returned to Africa after graduating from USC with my Bachelor's degree. "I sent you to America for an education, is this what they taught you? Anger? Hatred?" He had a tired look on his face as he turned and walked away. How could a few years in America have so transformed his little girl? Where was that understanding and communication that had made their relationship so special? Instead, there now stood an angry girl lashing out at the world. Was this the price of development? Maybe the ancestors had been right in not sending their little girls to schools; all it did was make them lose their sense of responsibility towards family, children and traditions. Jesus goes on quietly.

"Love is the first weapon we teach you to use here. You can't use your strength to destroy. You can't use your confidence to disconnect

> *those people you don't need or who oppose you."*

Why did I know He was going to bring up my CODE DELETE button? It isn't that I don't love people; I do. I do a lot of volunteer work. I love to help wherever I can. I disciple young women who are courageous enough to come under my leadership. I've been known to give generously to the homeless on the street. But...there are just a 'few' people that irritate me, and I don't see why I should keep them in my life especially when all they do is give me grief. We're all better off without each other, really, because one of us would likely turn up dead, most probably not me. I survived five brothers.

> *"You must fight that ego. You must stop operating in the flesh. You must become totally spiritual in your thinking. As long as you're not, you will continue to get discouraged, you will lack the power to do any kind of serious warfare. Without love, you have nothing. Why do you think My Church, so-called, is in such shambles? It's still all just a flesh dance.*
>
> *"Our purpose is to help other people become seekers and thinkers for themselves, but how will they see it if it isn't modeled for them? You can't cut off people just because they aren't as passionate as you are. Teach them. You will have to rely heavily on My patience. Even if you are given a tough message to deliver, it must always be delivered in love."*

Love. Love. It is inconceivable to me that I will ever love some of those on my deleted list with more than a superficial 'Christian love.' I could conceivably stop hating them, but love them...no. I won't lie.

> *"You have asked to follow in the footsteps of a man whose legacy was love. He was a leader of leaders, because he never did anything out of selfishness and empty conceit, but in everything he humbled himself and served his Lord and his fellow human beings with unmatched*

devotion. That's the standard."

Yes, You don't have to tell me...it was a first class standard. If I can even attain to twenty-five percent of what my father was, I'd be doing okay. He was a consummate peacemaker, a supreme diplomat, a leader of leaders, a man of true humility. He was just as comfortable speaking to an old woman on the roadsides of rural Uganda as he was with the President of Kenya. He was just as excited by the little children who crowded around him to hear his stories of Jesus as he was speaking to large audiences in expansive cathedrals.

"When a man's ways are pleasing to the Lord, He makes even his enemies to be at peace with him."
Proverbs 16:7.

My father's only enemy was the devil. His ministry centered around reconciliation, not only in Uganda, but around the world. His foundation was based solidly in his deep love for his Jesus. He was always ready to give a good word for Jesus.

That's the only thing I have to lean on. My love for Jesus. I can't even hope to come close to that standard without Him. If it worked for my father, then it will work for me. But...I still have so much self-doubt. I am too volatile. Jesus is quick to stop me from wallowing in self-pity.

"It's not that bad. You're headed in the right direction. Just memorize Proverbs 20:24, 'A man's steps are directed by the Lord.' We'll take care of the lessons one by one. You are aware that you have been given much, so I will expect much of you, but I will never demand more from you than you can bear. If you surrender yourself absolutely to me, you will be amazed at what you can do."

We're going to make it. I have complete trust in Jesus. I just have a feeling we're going to be coming back to the love lesson more often than not. But for right now, I raise my hands up to the Lord and I thank Him for being so gracious to me, for loving me so wonderfully. It is well with my soul. We move steadily on.

It's a challenge, this soldier training business. It's going to keep me on my toes. Jesus knows the intentions of my thoughts even before I know I'm going to think them. He knows all the people I have deleted and how I deleted them. He knows those I have killed in my spirit. Those I have wounded. We will follow His timetable, together we will press onwards. He will love and heal everyone through me. I await orders.

"Your assignment will start in the chicken pen.
Your purpose is to show them the way out.
You've been there. You know the way."

The chicken pen? No way. You're right, I've been there, I've talked to them, and the last thing they want to do is change from their wimpy, wishy-washy Christianity. They are too comfortable. They're just going to call me a heretic and throw me out. They already think I hallucinate all these things You tell me. Send me outside. There are so many hungry people out there. Better yet, send me home.

"Calm down. I'm just telling you what the
Father's plan is for you. You still have the
choice. If you have a better plan than His,
voice it, let's take a look at it, we'll reason
together."

That's very funny, Jesus. What better plan have I produced so far? My dreams flash before my eyes in vivid colour. I want to produce a string of successful films in Africa, for Africans, by Africans. I want to emancipate my brothers and sisters in every arena of their lives. I want to become very rich so I can feed every hungry child in Africa. Lost in thought, I am not aware of Jesus searching my motives. He sees the spirit of pride hovering above my head, and the spirit of unholy ambition trying to enter my mind. I am bothered by my thoughts, not so much the visions as the rewards I'm seeking. I look up to Him for help.

"Bind them, in my name. Don't let them have
any part in what the Lord has so graciously
done for you. God has given you good desires

and ambitions and the need to be recognized for what you can do well. Don't let the devil have any part in it. 'Put on the full armour of God, that you may be able to stand firm against the schemes of the devil.' Ephesians 6:11"

I bind the spirit of pride in the name of Jesus. I bind the spirit of unrighteous ambition in Jesus' name. Jesus moves closer to me sending the spirits scampering off. My thoughts become clearer. Just then a song comes on the radio. It's Whitney Houston's "All Alone." I start to weep uncontrollably. This was the first song I heard after my father's death and it still has the power to send me to pieces. I bend over, my face in my hands and I feel myself securely wrapped inside two strong, loving arms. I lean into a big, warm shoulder and I cry my heart out. Oh, Daddy, I miss you. I miss you so much. But I know you can see me, and I know you are proud of me. I'm going to continue the vision with the Lord's help. Just keep praying for me.

"...Weeping may remain for a night, but rejoicing comes in the morning." Psalm 30:5b.

"You turned my wailing into dancing; you removed my sackcloth and clothed me with joy, that my heart may sing to you and not be silent. O Lord my God, I will give you thanks forever." Psalm 30:11 & 12.

My tears and the memories of my father never fail to leave my heart lighter and my commitment to the Lord and to His vision for my life stronger. Tears have a way of breaking the heart, and Jesus has a way of mending that heart, refining it under His blowtorch, and then pouring His blessings inside. It is during these times that I renew my vows to God. Wherever You lead me, I will follow.

I am learning a very important lesson during these times of grief. "God is spirit, and those who worship Him must worship in spirit and truth." John 4:24. Not that Jesus hasn't explained all this before, but now it hits me in a fresh way. The Holy Spirit of God is the Commander-In-Chief of the Missionary Enterprise. It makes sense that a war that is in the spirit realm should be run by someone who's familiar with spiritual warfare, preferably God, the creator of heaven and earth. God makes His Holy Spirit available to all those who pledge allegiance to Him. If we report to Him, He will fight for us. We will have the full power of heaven behind us. We will be victorious. We shall have success. We shall have, "...love, joy, peace, patience, kindness, goodness, faithfulness, gentleness, self-control; all the things against which there is no law." Galatians 5:22. On our own...we are *nothing!* We are at the mercy of the schemes of the devil who is out to steal, kill, and destroy us. We will never rise above the level of mediocrity.

The chicken pen is full of people who think they are worshiping God, but are sacrificing at the altar of the flesh. I am not too excited about spending time with a bunch of people who fight tooth and nail to defend their lack of responsibility and sanctification. They fight to kill with their jealousy, their bitterness, their desire to keep sleeping...and I have no DELETE button. Well, I do, but I have been advised against using it; it's detrimental to my spiritual progress.

> **"'And I will ask the Father, and He will give you another Helper, that He may be with you forever...' John 14:16. Where there is a vision, there will be provision. All God requires from you is faithfulness. You ask Him for whatever you need, He will do it for you."**

I won't even touch that one. I used to debate Jesus on that issue, but now I realize it is just a matter of perspective; my will over His, nothing happens. His will over mine, everything happens. Now, we enter into another pasture. There are others warriors talking amongst themselves, joking, having a good time together. Some are singing worship songs. I like the spirit here. It is warm. I see a warrior standing by himself. Something draws me to him, or maybe it's Jesus leading me. I sense in him a real depth of passion and commitment to Jesus. I brace myself. Jesus has that look in His eyes again.

> *"You two have been called, and you have chosen to answer the call and go on from here."*

We keep our eyes fixed solidly on Him. To look around will only tempt us to call it a day and settle in this spiritual 'in-the-race-but-not-running-to-win' mode. Tested, but not to the maximum. Producing fruit, but not a hundred fold. Refined, but not transparent. I can't stop here. I don't think he can either. I wonder what his story is? Why the dedication?

> *"I am sick and tired of the nonsense that is going on in the chicken pen. You must go and tell them what time it is. If they ignore my warning and continue sleeping, I will be forced to spit them out and destroy their nation."*

I almost faint. I wonder if I am hallucinating? How does one tell that to the chickens without being pecked to death? It's one thing to try and motivate them, it's another to tell them they are doomed if they don't change their ways.

> *"Yes, they will accuse you of all sorts of things. Nothing they didn't do to me. But you knew it wasn't going to be easy. Take courage, 'For I have not given you a spirit of timidity, but of power and love and discipline.'" 2 Timothy 1:7.*

Jesus hands us both a set of clothes. Camo gear. I have finally made it. Warrior gear. Watch out world, here comes Sister Warrior. From now on we follow directions that say "Warrior Training." Neither one of us even looks to the other side to see if there are any signs to the chicken pen. We are headed that way anyway, but in the Missionary Enterprise, under the power and guidance of the Holy Spirit. We have only one thing on our agenda, to do the will of Him who sent us and to destroy all the works of the devil. We are going into the midst of wolves, we have been commanded to be wise as serpents and innocent as doves.

We are to take back all the territory that has been stolen from the kingdom of God, and to reclaim the lost generation, "For the Kingdom of God does not consist in words, but in power." 1 Corinthians 4:20. We are to be fishers of men, not of toys, not of houses, not of fame. We are to be fishers of men and women, boys and girls. All those who are lost, who are confused, who are sick and tired, who are stressed and just plain bored. Jesus wants them. He wants to give them peace. He wants to hear their song, the one only they can sing.

We are warriors, the only Christians that make the devil cower. We are warriors, we worship God and are without fear. We are warriors in the full armour of the Lord, from the Gospel of Peace to the Helmet of Salvation. We are warriors constantly in prayer and petition with the Spirit, asking for boldness to make known the mystery of the gospel of Jesus Christ. We are warriors, saved to the bone. Our Mission—to lift high the name of Jesus. HIGH! On wings like eagles.

Chapter 9

Choices

Out of my green folder marked "CHOICES", I read an excerpt of a conversation my sister and I had in 1989. It had then been three years since our father's death in March of 1986. I was thirty-one, recently married, and had been in America for thirteen years. She was ten years younger, had arrived in America the previous year, and was just starting college. She was very much an inspiration for this book because she represented the age group I wanted to reach.

She had agreed to give me an insight into her world. We sat across from each other at my small dining room table, me—with pen and paper, she—facing the Gestapo; being forced to dredge up memories she would rather forget.

"I'm glad I was born African," my sister said.

"Whether rich or poor?" I asked.

"That's where the problem rises," she replied reflectively.

"Do you know the meaning and purpose of life?" I asked.

"You've asked me that question before," she retorted, "Don't ask me again. I've thought about it and I seriously don't know what it's all about. Come to think of it, life is just education... struggling to make it. (pause) I've been thinking about it since the tragedy three years ago. Daddy, he worked hard, he was paid peanuts. He saved a little for the future, then he was killed. Now, what's the meaning?"

I choose to write a chapter on choices because to me that is how we find the meaning and purpose of life. Life is a series of choices. We are handed a set of circumstances and our job is to make the right choices. People who are constantly struggling in life are people who don't understand this concept. I've said many times, and I'll say it again, the battle is for our minds. Lose it there and you've lost it. The understanding of the power of our decisions makes us strong, no matter what deck of cards we were handed at birth, or what circumstances we face. We hold the keys to our future, for good, or for bad.

Most of the decisions that dictate how we live out the rest of our lives are forged in what has been called the "decade of decisions"—the ten years between the ages of fifteen and twenty-five. Whether you become a doctor or a paper pusher will be determined by the choices you make regarding your school grades during this critical decade. Whether you'll be happy or not will be determined by the quality of character you choose for yourself, and the type of people you surround yourself with—the winner crowd or the loser crowd. Once you pass the age of twenty-five, these patterns begin to set and become hard to break. Your choices will already be bearing fruit. You'll either be on a full scholarship pursuing a doctoral degree, or a single parent juggling three kids and a part-time job at K-Mart. Or worse—in prison, or dead.

Statistics show that most Christians make their decision for Christ during their teenage years. After the twenty-five year mark, the number of conversions drops dramatically. The effectiveness of your Christian life is also greatly determined by the level of commitment you make for Christ in this decade. If you leave the decade of decisions as a wishy-washy Christian, you are liable to remain a wishy-washy Christian the rest of your life. You will get married, have children and repeat the whole wishy-washy cycle. Children model what they see; or, if it's boring and irrelevant, they reject it altogether and head out into the world. We know many of these children as the lost generation.

This was my first mission field. After my father's death I made several futile attempts to manipulate my way back to Africa, but Jesus made it quite clear that He needed me in

America. He assured me that I would one day go back to Africa, but He wasn't saying when. Meanwhile, I had to be content with sporadic visits. It was pay-back time. Africa had received the gospel from missionary efforts; now the missionaries had lost their first love and needed African missionaries to show them how to once again dance the truth, and sing the love of God.

I braced myself for the American church. American Christianity, over a period of about thirty years, had been experiencing an exodus of true spiritual faith and was now scandalously littered with some of the most ineffective Christians ever to grace Christendom. Wishy-washy to the core. What the American church was in dire need of was a mighty outpouring of God, such as could break all those musty molds and revive them. A revival of this kind had not happened for...oh...let's say a very long time. So what was needed now was something akin to what happened in the valley of dry bones - nothing less. What America needed was a miracle.

Now in the late 1980s, I faced a church membership that consisted of dry bones, too proud to accept their neediness and too selfish to allow any fresh movement of God. They were notorious for screaming and fussing against anything that smacked of change. Any movement of the Spirit was squashed before it could disrupt their comfortable, lethargic religiosity. The convicting message of the gospel was avoided like the plague because to accept it meant that their bones would receive tendons, and flesh, and skin, and the Lord would command breath to enter them. Then they would have to stand up on their feet and become a vast army. That meant war. That meant suffering, and suffering for the cause of Christ was a concept they would rather inflict on others than incorporate in their own Christian experience. The church had become a therapeutic church, a place where people came to feel better. Repentance was a Greek word. Exhortation was a gift (ministry) of comfort and encouragement, not of exposing sin.

As I sought for guidance as to where the Lord wanted me to

set up shop and start working towards revival, opportunities came up for more convenient ministries, ones that would grant me popularity and prestige in Christendom, but no real accountability. Without Jesus what would they accomplish? What warrior wanted praise from chickens she did not particularly like or respect when she could get it from the God she adored? Besides, I wasn't given the gift of fraudulence. Neither, apparently, did I have the gift of diplomacy. I remember only too well the day when I put my blunt foot in my mouth and embarrassed my father, again. He had abruptly taken me aside and said with much annoyance, "The problem with you is that you're not diplomatic!" I didn't see any need to beat around the bush, but I was to learn in The Forge, over and over, that the truth had to be told in...yes, LOVE.

So... after visiting different churches, I plugged into the church which I had attended with my parents during the year my father studied at Fuller Theological Seminary in Pasadena. It was familiar; it was also close. You know the saying, "You can take the African out of Africa, but you can't take Africa out of the African." Punctuality was not one of my strengths. At least with this church, even if I left at the time the service started, I was guaranteed to be no more than ten minutes late. The main reason, of course, was because it was God's choice for me, and that became crystal clear as time went on.

I had visions. I had dreams. I was on a mission, a woman driven. I had the confidence that if a whole generation of American young people were to make the decision to leave the decade of decisions as warriors, on fire for God, then their fireworks would rock the world. We would put that embarrassing, fruitless record to rest. God's kingdom would once again rule in America, and I would go home. Mission accomplished. I figured all they needed was to have the 'want-to' and I was going to show them how. I was going to show them how to fight mediocre, spineless Christianity with everything in them. I would make them realize that life in the chicken pen was a fate worse than death.

It was war. I immediately joined the staff of the college group. Let's have rallies! Let's call for revival! Let's go! Let's go! Let's go! The wise college pastor listened to my enthusiasm and zeal, then told me gently, "Why don't you spend a few months getting to know the kids, and let them get to know you, then we can move from there." Wait? He wanted me to waste a few months before we could implement any of my visions!? What was I supposed to do until then?

I had become like my father. Waiting is to a warrior what walking is to a one-year-old. We want to run before we have learned how to walk properly. Waiting for God's timing is death...death to our impatience, death to our will and our sinful desires. It is accepting our weakness and our helplessness and allowing God's divine wisdom to lead us step by step, according to His perfect plan. Building precept upon precept.

As much as God loved my youthful fervor, it was impossible for Him to use if it was unbridled. It was a running joke in my family that my middle name was Kugumikiriza (Patience). They say I must have been at the end of the line when God was giving out patience, and by the time my turn came all He had left was the sign. Consequently, 'patience' was an all too familiar instrument in my forge experience.

I chose to wait. After a couple of months, I was given two girls to disciple. Then five. Soon I was leading small seminars and inviting the pastor's wife and various special guests to speak. Jesus could not have moved me into bigger responsibilities until He had tested my faithfulness in the little things, until I had learned a little more about humility and compassion.

After a year, I was an institution. I was asked periodically to give the message to the college group (over 120 strong) in their Sunday worship times. I went to everything, special evening events, Bible studies, staff meetings, special challenge groups, Christmas parties, retreats. And at all of them, I gave the challenge for people to move beyond learning about God to knowing Him. I was becoming a pest. I garnered the name 'Blowtorch.' But there was still no revival. I still saw no community. There was still no joy. I was frustrated.

During a particularly stuffy and phony staff meeting, I couldn't bear it any longer and burst out in protest. We were avoiding the one essential in Christianity—really knowing GOD. I walked out of that meeting and burst into tears. I had promised myself before that meeting not to open my mouth, and I held onto my promise pretty well until the Holy Spirit helped Himself to my vocal chords and let all heaven loose. Now I was the bad guy, and I didn't like the feeling. Yes, Jesus had warned me that the price of being a warrior was that you're often lonely, misunderstood, tired, frustrated. And yes, there were tears.

That was a miserable week. I didn't know where to go from there. Then I got the low-down. A staff leader told me that maybe my message was from God, but the messenger was questionable. I threw in the towel. I'd had it with America; I'd had it with the chickens. If they were going to be more concerned about the messenger than the message, then their fate was in their hands. They didn't even deserve to be invited to the table of opportunity. If they had passion only for mediocrity, then by all means I would get out of their way and let them have it. I started to wipe my feet. It was time to return to Africa. I needed to be in a real fellowship with real people, to see some authentic Christianity, feel some real joy, and hear about mighty answers to faithful prayer.

Meanwhile, I had other choices to make beginning with the more immediate, such as how to put food in my stomach and clothes on my back, to the more long-term decision of a life partner. The Lord had me in America, but I was not a resident. I was making it along on a professional work permit which had to be renewed every two years. Unable to get permanent sponsorship in the film industry, which was my area of training, I was reduced to doing temporary secretarial work in order to pay the rent.

I worked in just about every office environment in southern California, from an ophthalmologist's office, to mortgage companies, banks, department stores, a nurses aid agency, studios, restaurants, tool companies, you name it, (that's a book in itself). It always made me feel better to remember that Paul had to make tents to pay his rent. A Pharisee of Pharisees making tents! He could have been the president of the grandest theological college of his time, but the Lord had him making tents. Typing didn't seem so bad. The money... well?

Soon, it became too expensive to pay the lawyers and my work permit lapsed. Immigration lawyers were suggesting I get married to an American citizen, anyone with whom I could come into agreement, and get my green card. Everyone was doing it. Then I could get a job anywhere and make the kind of money I deserved.

I fell on my knees before the Lord. I didn't want to go against His will, but He hadn't intervened. I didn't see any other way out. If He wanted me in America, then He should make it possible for me to stay in America legally, otherwise I wanted to go home. But I couldn't go home. I didn't have a dime for the air fare. I had no prospects for a job. My mother was still in exile in Kenya, and even her situation was tenuous since Kenya was sending Ugandans back now that the war was over. I was in America, stuck between a rock and a hard place, exercising every last bit of faith I had.

There was no denying by now that what Ken and I felt for each other was love. He had seen me through the worst period of my life, and we had developed a very deep friendship. We liked being together. But...he had been raised a Catholic. He was not born again. I was a warrior in the Lord's army. I could not be unequally yoked. I could not even date him, at least we couldn't acknowledge it as such. "Unequally yoked?" he asked, the first time I told him; "What's that?"

All my efforts to this point to bring him into the knowledge of Christ had consisted of one Bible story after another. He had accompanied me to church on several occasions, and I visited his Catholic church which he attended quite regularly. But there was no light at the other end of the spiritual tunnel. This was not particularly alarming to me at first, because I had no intentions of marrying him. I had no intentions of ever marrying a white man. His salvation was for his own soul. I wanted him to know Jesus.

He startled me one day, as we were discussing my immigration situation. He suggested we get married so I could get my green card. Not that the thought hadn't occurred to me; of course, desperation explores every possibility, but this was only entertained in lawyer's offices when they asked if I had a boyfriend. I had never really thought of marrying Ken as a possibility, and it shocked me that he did. From the looks of it, everything seemed fine, after all...we did care for each other. All things being equal, we were very suited for one another. But, it was wrong in the sight of God.

I grappled with that issue as intently as I grappled with the issues of Ken's race and spiritual status. All three went against my grain. I tried the marriage idea on a few close friends and they encouraged me to do it; after all, Ken was not doing it for money but for love. I pushed the limit as far as I could, even contemplated a date, but I knew I could never commit that grievous a sin to my Lord. I would rather walk and swim back to Africa and live in a village, selling mangoes on the roadside (to American tourists) for the rest of my life.

I had asked for uncommon obedience. I would ask for continued patience and trust. I needed to stay on course. My will would only throw me seriously off track. Besides, Jesus was with me. "For I know the plans that I have for you," declares the Lord, "plans for welfare and not for calamity, to give you a future and a hope." Jeremiah 29:11.

Now, however, the subject had been brought up. What were we going to do about our relationship? Where was it going? Seeing my renewed commitment to wait upon the Lord and let Him work out my situation in His time, Ken embarked on a serious search for this God to whom I had so powerfully committed my life. "And you will seek Me and find Me, when you search for Me with all your heart." Jeremiah 29:13. He studied the Bible, listened to Christian radio, attended church regularly, searching.

In the past, young men had 'become' Christians in order to date me, but not Ken. Like me, he had not been given the gift of fraudulence. He lived by the truth, and the truth here was that as long as he was not born-again, there was no hope of us getting married. Realizing the depth of our feelings I went to the Lord in prayer, my way.

This wasn't meant to be, dear Lord. I can't marry a white man. Besides, I don't think an interracial marriage could be your will for me; You promised You would eventually send me back home to live, remember? What would I say to my fellow Africans with a white husband in tow? Moreover, he isn't a Christian anyway, so please take these feelings away from me. You can bring my brown, African man and I can fall in love with him. I'd like him to be six feet tall, medium build, and a diplomat so I can be the hostess with the mostest and entertain royalty, (the list was fairly long). Of course, he has to be a warrior. Together we will change Africa.

All that praying and dreaming didn't change the fact that I was hopelessly in love with Ken. He had all the qualities I was looking for in a man; he had a good heart and a good soul, not to mention the fact that his combination of dark hair and blue eyes made him very pleasing to the eye. He just happened to be white and still searching spiritually. What was a woman to do? I had to make a choice. I continued to pray.

Meanwhile, back on the church front, I tried to pull a Jonah stunt, but after a short gig in deep blue water (I assume it was blue—it's dark inside that big fish), I reluctantly returned to the college group. I kept plugging away, opening my big mouth and calling for revival until I couldn't call anymore. At each meeting I promised myself I would shut up and go through the motions, but I didn't belong to myself anymore, I belonged to the Holy

Spirit. He was my Commander in Chief. When He had a message, it had to be given. Then I got pelted, more from my own insecurities and impatience than actual rejection from the people I was trying to serve and serve with.

One semester our focus was on 'Knowing God and Making Him Known,' but I was appalled at some of the suggested topics for study. Most of them skirted the deeper spiritual issues in favor of a more life-centered focus. I wrote up suggested new topics for review...mainly, 'Knowing God.' Without that basis, I insisted, we were toiling in vain. We couldn't make God known if we didn't know Him ourselves.

I was convinced that the Lord wanted revival to start in that college group and I stuck with it through several pastoral administrations, carrying the same, consistent message—revival.

On the work front, I was still working in various temporary situations and writing on the side. I knew then that if I was ever to get into the filmmaking business I would have to write my way into it. I had it all mapped out. I would write a book for young people, because my father's greatest interest had been to challenge the rising generation into practical, moral obedience to Christ. Then, when the book was a best seller, I, like my father, would travel around the world (particularly in Africa), speaking to stadiums full of young people, and old people, calling them to revival. Then I would finish the documentary I was working on as a tribute to my father. Then I would write and produce a theatrical movie on his life...all this while married to my diplomat and entertaining royalty. I was, indeed, heir to my father's mantle. The word 'rest' had mysteriously vanished from my vocabulary.

One late December day, 1987, Ken called me and in excitement told me he had accepted Christ. I was ecstatic, bewildered, hurt, doubtful, all at the same time. Ecstatic—because we had both prayed for it, and he was so happy to finally know this Jesus whom I had been talking about. His mind was finally opened to things of the Spirit. My pride was hurt, because it was Dr. Charles

Swindoll over the radio whom Jesus had given the words to open Ken's heart, not me. I was bewildered, because it took away my last excuse not to discuss marriage. I was doubtful, because I didn't want to play with things that were spiritual. I wanted the real deal, but it is easy to see Jesus in a person, and in Ken 'light had come into a beautiful bulb.'

That light then shone on an area in my life whose time had come. I had to deal with my racial prejudice. In Jesus there was no unrighteousness and He did not keep company with evil. His grace had covered me until now, while I learned other important lessons. Now, progress had stalled. I had reached the 'Love-Thine-Enemies Station' in the Forge. Very few ever proceeded beyond this point, three to five percent to be exact. In fact, only those who were truly possessed by their love for Jesus ever even dared to step into this Forge, and only the truly humble, truly selfless, ever stepped out the other end. This was not the place for people who were opposed to heat and long journeys.

I was pretty sure Jesus would have to take me through it kicking and screaming...if I ever stepped inside. I wanted to hang on to my bitterness and my anger. I wanted to call it righteous anger; after all, we had been wronged and we needed to right those wrongs, not turn the other cheek. I sat outside, practicing selectivism in my Bible reading. I kept hoping that 'some' of my prayers for my African man had been heard and were under serious consideration. That would help me sweep my prejudice under the carpet, and maybe Jesus would look at all the wonderful work I was doing for Him and forgive me that one little, minor, insignificant s...s...sin.

Maybe Jesus would have forgiven me (and allowed me to stay stuck on that bench outside that forge), but Ken wasn't so understanding. He wanted to know why, if I loved him, was I letting the issue of race deprive us both of a wonderful life together? After all, wasn't I the one who preached that life was spiritual, all other things didn't matter? Yes, and I believed it. But I was a hypocrite.

I couldn't bring myself to do the things I knew in my mind, and about which I spoke so eloquently.

Part of me wasn't really sure there was an answer to black anger. As much as I loved Jesus, I didn't know how to trust Him with this. I didn't want to become a racial wimp by giving God control of the vengeance. So far I had seen no vengeance and my people had been praying a mighty long time. I also felt if I married a white man I'd be watered down and lose my strength, my blackness, my pride. I still saw my strength in standing beside a strong African man. I was looking for an image like my father's, a man I would be proud to stand beside.

I prayed, and hoped against hope. I was thirty, and no African man was in sight. Several times I tried to stop seeing Ken. Talk about misery. Without Ken I was pitiful. He was the only one who tried to understand the methods of my madness; everyone else thought I was possessed. He was the one who hugged me when I walked out of those meetings, wounded in the struggle for the souls of the college group. I needed him. I loved him. There had never been, nor did I see any hope of, anyone who would captivate me like he did. But...I was often embarrassed to be seen with him in certain sections of town, not because he wasn't gorgeous, I saw those girls in waiting—ready to pounce the minute I stepped out of the picture, but because I felt like I was selling out. I was letting my people down.

There were lessons to be learned still outside this forge. First, why was I really stuck there? Was it because I really couldn't forgive white people, or that I just didn't want to? Why did I think they weren't deserving of my forgiveness? They had God's. Was colour really so important that I was willing to give up a good man (a rare commodity in these days) simply because of the colour of his skin? Did I really care that much about what other people thought of me?

Then I heard a Christian psychologist make a statement that shook me up: Denial is the most powerful drug known to mankind.

The opposite of truth was not lies...it was denial, because you couldn't get to the lies until you had done a tango with denial. I had always been a strong supporter of an intelligent Christianity. A Christianity that embraced the truth and adamantly fought against denial. A Christianity that made choices from the facts not fiction. A Christianity that engaged the mind. A transparent Christianity that pushed for excellence and progress...by any means necessary, even the cemetery. Now I was to expand that thought to the heart. An intelligent Christianity without heart was merely a clanging cymbal. It was a Christianity in denial. It was a Christianity benched. The Gospel without Jesus.

There I sat, refusing to engage the heart when it came to white people. Jesus sat quietly beside me. That's what I loved most about Him—He never left me. I felt no condemnation from Him. I was still wonderfully loved, I just didn't have a message for anyone. How could I preach about peace and reconciliation when I was harboring such hatred and bitterness in my own heart?

I didn't know what steps I was going to take, and I didn't really believe it was possible for me to love white people, but there was one thing I knew, I couldn't stay benched forever. I had heard that exciting things went on inside the "Loving Thine Enemies" station. Men and women literally developed wings and took off like eagles, doing mighty exploits in the name of Jesus. I had lived for most of my life watching such a person do things I couldn't comprehend in my finite, human mind. Somehow my father had found the secret to seeing beyond the colour and had been freed to great service for Jesus.

Jesus. Seeing Him sitting beside me unable to bless the people He wanted to bless through me brought me to my senses. My first loyalty was to Him. So I set out to hit denial with the truth. That was the only hope I had of breaking through the denial-caused dysfunction that was impeding my progress and blocking the spiritual artery to my heart. I had to stop refusing to grant the truth. In Jesus, I could love anybody, I just had to have the 'want to.' Yes, I'd heard that a few times, maybe even out of my own mouth. Was the message just for 'them' or could I benefit from it myself?

I had only one life to live and there was no reason to live it by what other people said or thought, or to be caught up in bitterness and superstition when I had a good heart and a sound mind, not to mention full access to the Throne of God. I was not a follower of men, I was a follower of Jesus Christ. I had to be an example, set the standard. Only Truth believed in by both my mind and my heart would set me free to love all people the way I knew Jesus wanted me to love them.

The popular pop group 'En Vogue' has a great line in one of their songs, "Free your mind, the rest will follow." God had guaranteed that every earnest, open-minded seeker would find Him. Now, I had to hand Him my heart filled with hate in exchange for His heart filled with love. I had a lot at stake. If Ken was truly God's choice for me, was I going to let prejudice rob me of such a gift? Was I going to let all my dreams and visions for young people around the world be deflated by an inability to make a choice for love?

I took a deep breath, stood up, took Jesus' hand and turned towards the door. Behind that door was the legendary blowtorch, the mother of them all, the only flame strong enough to engage the heart and produce that kind of love. The undeniable fire of the Love of God in Christ Jesus. The one that filled hearts with joy and made faces glow. That was my first choice.

I was going in—for the love of God. The love of Jesus. The love of a man. For the love of college students, and the love of my fellow human beings. I wanted to be just like my father. I was going to learn how to become a real donkey for Jesus. Whatever little demons of self I was still holding onto were about to meet the instrument that would deal with them according to the purposes God had for me. One day, people would know me not only for my zeal and energy, but also for my love.

Chapter 10

One Flame

On the day I was born in Kampala, Uganda, God had already planned out my life. He had already planned the life of another precious child who was soon to be born in Elizabeth, New Jersey. From the moment of our conception, He weaved us delicately in our mothers' wombs and put into those two little hearts a love for Him and a love for one another, though both loves would not be experienced until we were in our twenties, and at quite a cost.

When I entered the 'Love-Thine-Enemies' Forge I had to come in backwards with my eyes closed. Then I crouched by the wall, my face in my hands. I couldn't look at the Light, it was too much for me. I was too ashamed. My father used to say that the image that turned his heart to God was of the horror of being ushered into the presence of the Living God all covered with dust. That's how I felt when I saw my attitudes and sins in the Light of God. I was all covered in dust.

I had been trying to buck the system. Now, as I looked at the reasons why I was not in agreement with the choice of colour of the one chosen for me, they all seemed so petty. Who cared if he wasn't a diplomat, or chocolate brown, or African? He was six feet tall and the most wonderful man on planet Earth. Jesus began to show me how God had been preparing our two lives for each other.

Since childhood, Ken had had this tremendous fascination for the world, but particularly Africa. His parents had subscribed to National Geographic for him, and each month he would scour the magazines for stories on Africa. He would also research topics of interest and write weekly reports which he filed neatly into several large folders. He knew the names of all the countries in Africa and their capitols. He knew more animals by name on the continent of Africa than I did, and I was the African with a Master's degree in Africa Area Studies. All he had left to do was actually visit.

Now Ken and I shared Jesus. He joined the church, made a public confession of his faith in Jesus and was baptized. Together, we placed our relationship in the hands of God and committed ourselves to serious prayer. If God wanted us together, He would confirm it in our hearts. It wasn't an easy decision for either one of us. Ken had no personal hangups about the colour of my skin, but he knew his parents' feelings would be strongly negative. I knew my mother would look at character over colour, but I had personal hangups about his colour.

We decided to seek counseling from Christian sources. We attended conferences and seminars which dealt on the matter of race and interracial relationships. We learned about all the interracial marriages in the Bible, including how God punished Aaron and his sister for ridiculing Moses' marriage to a Cushite woman. Over and over we heard that being unequally yoked referred strictly to spiritual inequality. But I was caught up in my image. As a future leader in Africa, I couldn't see a white man beside me. I could sense Jesus getting impatient with me. I was deliberately missing His point. I couldn't see God's plan to use Ken and me as a powerful message to a world caught up in severe racial tensions. I didn't need the extra burden. But God wasn't going to let me cower in the corner forever.

I will never forget the day He drove the message home into my heart. The saying 'pride goes before a fall' took on a whole new meaning. It was at a Navigators' Conference. Ken and I had enrolled in several seminars, and by the afternoon, I was becoming bored and impatient. I hadn't really heard anything unique, and there were too many people, ordinary, lack-luster Christians, the type that depressed me to no end. Leaders stood up and gave expositories on their subjects, people asked questions from their wimpy, mostly white, materialized spiritual angst, looking for a magic formula. Then we prayed and moved on to the next seminar.

I was ready to go home before the last seminar, but a good friend and discipler challenged me to stay. I forget the exact name of the seminar, but it had something to do with unity in Christian service. I figured they would work their way through their pseudo-Christian love talk, then we would listen to some more spiritual dysfunction, then pray, and we would have wasted another precious hour.

Ken and I sat as far from the action as possible with the intention of just observing. However, involvement was the motivating force behind our leader and he soon had everyone out of their seats and standing around a table. Four people had been chosen to play a game and were seated at the table. In front of each were various brightly coloured pieces of wood to be fit together to make squares. They were to pass on to each other whichever pieces they did not need. The goal was four perfect squares.

I stood there thinking how very stupid the game was. It was simple. Just pass the yellow pieces to one person, the blue to another, the red to another, and the green to another. Why were the four players trying to put red and green pieces with yellow and blue pieces? I so much as even voiced my opinion to a few people close to me. But, as I stood there feeling more and more sheepish, four squares began to take form, each made up of all the four colours.

We sat back in our seats. I was amazed at how something so simple had taken on such a twist. Using different coloured pieces to make a perfect square would never have been my way of doing it, but it was God's. This was the basis of unity in Christian service. God put all colours together as He saw fit. He was less concerned with our skins than He was with our hearts. In His eyes, we were all equal. Why then was I so bent over colour? I knew then that I had a better chance of being hit by lightning than of God making me fall out of love with Ken, and then fall in love with my very own made-to-order African diplomat.

This called for some serious introspection. I sat up and Jesus took my hand, his voice gentle, reassuring.

"I know how you feel."

It was true. Jesus knew all my thoughts. He knew my pain. He understood my hurt, my black anger. We sat together, alone on the beach at Santa Monica, looking out at the big blue ocean, watching the beautiful sunset, marveling at God's creation. I had to break. I wanted to be rid of my anger and hatred. I didn't want to live in hate any more. If Jesus really could heal me from this, I was willing to work with Him. With Him I was safe, I could pour out my feelings knowing He wouldn't judge me or leave me. I believed that with every tear He would gently wipe away, He would also wipe away the bitterness and resentment against white people that festered in my heart.

What they did to us was so unfair, Lord. What they are continuing to do to us is unpardonable. Why should they live so comfortably while we live like rats in the cesspools and the ghettos of the world? They deprive us of the fundamentals of life and then spit at us for not being able to get ourselves out from under their oppression. They refuse to rent us apartments in decent neighborhoods, and underpay us at jobs unfit for humans, then overcharge us on all we purchase. They call us names, consider us less than human and practice every injustice against us known to man. How are we supposed to take that without being angry? How can I watch all the suffering they have caused my people and not be angry? How can I continue to listen to reports of black people being beaten and killed by white policemen in South Africa, or the deaths of our young black men in the iron streets of Los Angeles, and not get furious?

"Why do you think you weren't born in South Africa or the United States? You would have

**gotten yourself killed by now with that hot
temper of yours. Here you will learn how to be
angry but not hate, for hate will only destroy
you, and you will forfeit the wonderful plan
God has for your life. You will learn how to use
that anger positively, not destructively. The
lessons you learn here will be the foundation
of your own ministry of peace and reconciliation. The bottom line is still..."**

Don't say it. Don't say it. I know. Love! The first thing I had
to do was release Ken. He was not responsible for what had happened in Africa. He was just as concerned about it as I was and
seemed genuinely excited about the prospect of spending significant time in Africa.

Up to that point, I had not told Ken I loved him. He believed
I loved him, but he had not heard it articulated. I was quick to call
people to war, but didn't know how to say "I love you." One
evening, on the way to dinner at our favourite restaurant, I said it
quickly. His face lit up and he said, "I heard that. I heard that." I
was embarrassed. I couldn't bring myself to say it again, but it
had felt good to eventually put words to my feelings. I had
bridged a tremendous gap. I had finally admitted my vulnerabili-
ty. In the weeks that followed it became easier for me to tell him
how much he meant to me.

One day Ken ventured into the territory of marriage, trying to
find out how I felt about it. I laughed uneasily and pulled my eyes
away from his. I couldn't discuss that yet. He didn't press the
issue. He knew I hadn't become angry overnight, I needed time to
work through the issues. Despite the personal hurdles we had
overcome so far, I still saw him as belonging to the group of the
oppressors. He still benefitted from the system, I did not. He was
privileged, I was not. I wasn't sure he really understood my pain.
There was still a lot he had to know about what life was like for
a black person, particularly the African woman who was at the
bottom of the global totem pole.

At first it was difficult for him to really listen, to really understand. It was risky to step out of his white world that had been effectively inoculated from the black man's hurt and pain, and I didn't blame him. Why should he? He could live anywhere he wanted, go anywhere he pleased. Isn't that what we're all looking for in life - a good, comfortable life?

I remember my father asking me one day after I had asked him to stop supporting me. "But why do you have to suffer if you don't have to?" I was a writer, I had reasoned, I needed to feel pain. How could I write without having felt pain? Now Ken, by virtue of his wanting to marry a black woman, had to feel my pain. He had to really understand it, not with a clinical, calculated effort, but a deep, practical, heart-wrenching, eye-opening revelation in a spirit of sincerity and truth. This was authentic Christianity and humanity.

I believe God could have applied a Holy Spirit touch to my heart and instantly healed me of my anger, but He didn't. He couldn't. How would Ken and I lead others into healing if we hadn't traveled the road ourselves? How would we know the issues both sides brought to the table if we avoided confrontation?

It wasn't easy for Ken to listen to my anger towards the white race, particularly the white man, but we had no future together as husband and wife if he didn't really understand my pain. He would be stuck in his world telling me something simplistic like "Let's just forget the past and move on." Or my personal favourite, "We're tired of being blamed for your problems." He needed to feel it, to understand it, to realize that racial hatred needed serious healing, not platitudes. Serious healing could only occur if the white race really understood our pain and reached out in love and repentance. Massive doses of self-love were essential, but to complete the healing would take for the two sides to come together, for there was no fundamental renewal for one without the other. Jesus was coming back for a unified Church. That is where our strength lay.

It wasn't easy for me to accept that most of our suffering was going on unfelt by the majority of the white race. They were safely tucked away in suburbia, anesthetized by their comfort and privilege, wishing those of us without privilege would collectively develop amnesia, forget our wretched past and be content with our poverty, our crime, our violence. It was amazing to me that many white people actually believed that black people had the same freedoms they had, and that black people caused their own problems by being lazy. It was painful to hear the stereotypes passed down through the generations and to see how this had aided the general white population in their denial of the truth. The truth cost too much. Responsibility. Sharing. Love!

These discussions that Ken and I had were never confrontational because we had Jesus in our midst, listening, mediating, illuminating. We were not there to convert each other, or even to heal one another. We were there to listen to each other, to support one another, and in thus doing we allowed Jesus to do His work of restoration in our hearts and minds. Soon Ken was able to really look deeply into my eyes and see inside my heart. As his defenses melted away, he was able to see how he, as a passive beneficiary of the system, was actually playing a role in perpetuating that hurt.

As I released some of that anger to a listening, understanding white ear, my need to constantly be on the offensive dissolved. I was able to look at history realistically and accept the fact that black men were killing black men in unprecedented numbers around the globe. I conceded that illiterate, selfish, gun-toting buffoons had taken over from the colonialists and were now pillaging Africa and sending it into such economic and social decline it was going to take a miracle to restore it. I admitted that the gun and the Bible were not the things that had killed my father, but the black hand that pulled the trigger. I knew I could no longer hide behind colonialism. I did not need to play victim anymore; I could move on to healing, then on to freedom, then work towards change in true love and forgiveness.

I began to feel a real oneness with Ken. I knew that the missing pieces of the puzzle had been found, at least for now. What we still had to learn we would do together. God had put the two of us together to fulfill a very special purpose, to build a platform for peace, black and white together in real human fellowship flowing from true brokenness and repentance. To lose the possibilities God had for us would not only be tragic to Africa but to America as well. I recognized that we could not change history, but we had to change the future. On Valentine's Day, 1988, I handed Ken a card. He read it almost in disbelief. "If the offer is still standing, I would be very privileged and proud to be your wife."

As was usual with my honeymoon experiences in the forge, I didn't have long to enjoy the freedom I found in my choice for love. I immediately entered into a testing period that would reverberate in my system for many years to come. Ken had not wanted to tell his parents about the status of our relationship until he knew I was solidly with him. As he had anticipated, the reaction was very negative.

I need to state here that my relationship with my family-in-law has been healed over the past few years and I am loathe to go back and dig up the pain, but if I am to write a chapter on reconciliation and unity, then I must delve into some of the dynamics of what has been the biggest lesson on reconciliation I have learned to date. It is to the glory of the wonder-working power of Jesus Christ that I share these personal details, and for the future of race relations in the twenty-first century.

It was easy to love Ken, I had even resolved to accept my big, oftentimes chilly, predominantly white church, but to ask me to love and forgive a couple of people who thought I was not good enough to marry their son because of the colour of my skin, was to put too much pressure on my fledgling commitment. I was willing to give them a break; after all, anyone who raised a son such as Ken deserved the benefit of the doubt. However, when I heard that we were supposed to have orchestrated the whole thing simply to hurt them, I lost it. I could not believe such arrogance. Why would I waste my entire future to hurt two white people I hardly knew? And what they called 'pain' was simply pride, an inability to face their friends with the fact that their son was going to marry a 'black' person. I resorted to the only thing I knew in order to cope, I reached for my CODE DELETE button and pushed it. The less I heard about them and their pain, the better.

Ken and I were totally assured that our marriage was God's plan. My mother had visited California on several occasions, and in her eyes Ken could do no wrong. She assured me that my father would have been in total agreement. Ken was just like my father in everything that really mattered. That was good enough for me. We set a date and went about planning our wedding.

During the course of the eight months before the wedding, I discovered that my CODE DELETE button which had worked very effectively when I was single, didn't function so well now that I was part of a team. I couldn't just delete my mate's parents. Ken was caught between two sides he loved dearly, being forced to choose between the two. It was unfair, and I hated to see him go through it, but I felt powerless to help him; after all, what could I do? I couldn't change my colour.

We tried to reason with them. We bought books on biracial children to assure them that our children wouldn't be deformed or socially disadvantaged. We established the fact that we would never live in the Midwest, we would stay on the more liberal West Coast for as long as we were in America. All of a sudden, my education was invalid, my 'first-class' upbringing was insignificant, my goals and achievements were unimportant, my Christianity was a cult. I began to see just how blinding racism was. All they could see was my dark skin and the shame of this happening to them.

I found myself back in the muck and mire of hatred and anger. I couldn't believe it. I felt like all my work had been chucked aside and I had to relearn this lesson all over again...

from the beginning. I blamed my in-laws for this obstacle in my spiritual progress. Thankfully, they lived in the Midwest, far enough away that I could pretend they didn't exist. But I was a team now, whatever affected Ken affected me. The phone calls from and to his parents would send him to the roof, then his sisters got involved, then soon all sorts of rumours were flying.

Seeing how much it upset me, Ken developed a policy of not telling me what was going on and what was being said; however, there were times when I was dragged into it by one or the other of the in-laws wanting to voice their opinion directly to me. I did not relish these incidents, because my short fuse was unpredictable and they always managed to dance on my last nerve. "Do you know what you are doing to our family?" Me? Or the God-given, God-designed colour of my skin? It was all I could do not to unleash venom that would have destroyed any chance of reconciliation in the future. Instead, I unleashed it to Ken, and he listened to as much as he could, but I had to learn how to be sensitive. After all, these were his parents, 'two of the nicest people you'd ever want to meet.'

"Nice" was not a word I wanted to associate with Ken's family at that time. I had my own set of adjectives. I applied for grace. I would try not to retaliate if Jesus would just cover me with His grace as I struggled with my inability to love.

> *"Now you know why this is considered the ultimate love station. As you can see there aren't that many people who are willing to love on this level. That's why there are endless wars everywhere. But you know what to do. Just hand it over to me. Let me take it. Let me love them through you."*

I wanted to. If not for my sake, for Ken's sake. If I could learn how to forgive, and maybe even understand them, then this whole thing would be so much easier on him, on us. As it was, he was becoming increasingly alarmed at how much I actually hated his parents. Everything in our lives was fine, my family was behind us, our friends were happy for us, Californians didn't see anything abnormal with us, people didn't stop and gawk at us. Our only problem in the area of race now stemmed from two people who were paranoid about what everybody else was going to think.

> *"'And forgive us our debts, as we also have forgiven our debtors.' Matthew 6:12. You, my dear, have conveniently forgotten how much you have been forgiven, and how much forgiveness you still need in this area of prejudice. Maybe you need a refresher course on Matthew 18:21-35. How many times must you forgive? Seventy times seven. Otherwise you are only as good as that slave who was forgiven much by his master, but was then unwilling to forgive his fellow servant for a much smaller debt. Should you not also have mercy on your fellow slaves, even as I have had mercy on you?"*

So we were going there, were we? It was uncanny how Jesus always managed to turn the spotlight on me. I had been forgiven much. This matter of prejudice did not exist in terms of just black and white for me. I was African, which meant I belonged to a tribe, (ethnic group, if you prefer). Tribalism was a cancer that was tearing that beautiful continent apart. Uganda alone boasted of people groups which spoke over thirty different languages and many more dialects. One of the two most widely spoken African languages in Uganda was Luganda (the other being Swahili), the language of the Baganda, the largest and most dominant group. To get a better perspective a bit of history is necessary.

By the arrival of the first Europeans in 1862, the Kingdom of Buganda was already at the level of organization that surprised the English explorers. The King was elected by a royal council to succeed his dead father, the former monarch. Then he chose his counselors, his Chief of Armed Forces, and the Gabunga (Admiral) in charge of war canoes. The Buganda monarchy was absolute. The Kingdom of the Baganda was rich and powerful.

During the period of colonialism, the British colonial policy only reinforced and consolidated the power of the Baganda by making Buganda the center of their Protectorate. Buganda became the center of political and economic power with the seat of government located in the capitol city of Kampala. The Baganda were given a higher status than the rest of the tribes, and were afforded greater educational and job opportunities, their incomes were often ten to twenty times higher than the rest of the country. I was from that group. I had grown up believing in our superiority over all the other groups.

Living in Kampala, I had been raised with the same privileges in Africa that I despised the white race for enjoying in America. I had been guilty as a Southerner of not wanting my children to grow up and marry a Northerner. The American experience helped me to re-evaluate my attitude on tribalism. In America I was a minority. I could not practice the arrogance and indifference that comes from being part of the majority group. Here I could only accept the crumbs that were thrown at me, much like what the minority groups had put up with in Uganda until Northerners like Milton Obote and Idi Amin snapped and took over power by force, plunging Uganda into a twenty-year nightmare.

In America, I had asked for and received forgiveness from Jesus for my role in perpetuating that tribal hatred. I now understood the pain of the minority groups in Uganda, I had walked in their shoes for a moment. I began to see Ugandans not as categories—Northerners, Westerners, Easterners or Southerners—but as people, my brothers and sisters, all belonging to the same nation, each and every one of us equal under God and deserving of equal justice. In gratitude to God, I had resolved to work for reconciliation. But now here I was, having been forgiven much, yet totally unwilling to forgive those who were committing no greater sin than I had been guilty of for so many years. Then there was the black-brown issue. I was still guilty of an inability to love Asian Indians from my heart. I resented their presence in Africa, their economic domination, and their disrespect for Africans. I still thought Idi Amin had done a great service in expelling them all in the 1970s, if nothing else. If my son were to bring home an Indian girl I would probably do no less than what my in-laws were doing to me. Jesus' bright light was pointed directly at my hypocrisy.

The heat in the Forge was becoming unbearable. I didn't see how I was going to open my hands and release to Jesus my need to strike back. I wanted to continue writing letters so scathing that had I sent them they would have cut them open and laid their guts out. I was intent on holding on to my pride. I wanted to continue hating more than I wanted to forgive and love. Love cost too much, and they didn't deserve it.

Christians have often been accused of using Jesus as a crutch. Wrong. I didn't need a crutch. Jesus was my stretcher. I was out for the count on this matter. There was a long period of time when the communication lines with Ken's immediate family were severed, except his older sister who believed in the course of true love. Then we received news that Ken's parents were not coming to the wedding. Grace had to abound as never before. When they sent us two round trip tickets to Indiana to 'talk face to face' I laughed. All they wanted to do was talk us out of getting married. I didn't need to waste my time on that. Ken and I were getting married no matter what anybody said, even if God was to be our only witness. Besides, the wedding was less than two months away and I was busy.

It was my mother, my own flesh and blood, that convinced me to go into what I perceived then as the lions' den. She told me I owed it to Ken to give his parents this chance. I remember the words Ken told me before our plane took off; he had taken my hand securely in his and said, "If I walk out, follow me and we'll take the first flight back." We were a team. As long as I was with him everything would be alright. Contrary to pulling us apart, these experiences were drawing us together in a very special way.

Nothing much was accomplished during those three days, just a rehashing of all the stuff that had transpired over the past months.

They were no closer to accepting us than we were to changing our minds. They were stuck in 'convention,' and we were on the road called 'progress.' Maybe I managed to assure them that I had no ulterior motive for marrying their son, and that I didn't have any children tucked away in a ghetto somewhere, but beyond that they still saw me as a black 'person.' I was still a category, not a human being. Maybe I got to understand the Mid-west mentality a little better, but I hated it no less.

To their credit, they made it to the wedding and witnessed what must have been their worst nightmare. I was happy for Ken that they were there to share the day with him, and I sensed my heart melting a degree or two. But again that was short-lived. Ken and I had agreed not to start a family for at least a couple of years. We needed to pay off some of our wedding debts before children came into the picture. Well, God had another agenda.

A month after our wedding my doctor confirmed that I was pregnant. We couldn't believe it. We had taken every precaution. Ken didn't know how to tell his parents. When he finally did, they disconnected us for several months. Again, we had supposedly done this to spite them. With all the birth control available, how could we have allowed such a thing? My hand was now constantly on my DELETE button. I didn't need that mess. I had to concentrate on producing a happy, healthy baby, I had no time for stress of that nature. Neither, apparently, did Ken. He now had a family of his own to take care of, and that was his first priority.

Well, the short of it is that Jordan was born ten months after we were married. He was big, healthy and beautiful. And as grandchildren are apt to do, he melted his grandparents hearts. We started receiving presents and cards from Indiana. We were invited back for Christmas. I went through the motions, but still did not hear the words I longed to hear. No one admitted to hurting me. No one said they were sorry for 'my' pain. Was I supposed to just drop the past and head into the future as though it all didn't matter? They were working on resolving their issues, there were therapy sessions and support groups, and I was supposed to be patient with them until they were able to fully accept me. But who was going to help me deal with my issues? My hurt pride? My dignity that had been stomped on? The negative words that kept ringing in my ears? Did I not have a soul as a black person?

Did my opinion of their treatment of me not matter simply because I was black? Was the equation tilted so unfairly in their minds that I didn't warrant a "We are sorry?" Apparently not. I refused to accept their presents, because I could not receive them in the spirit intended. I could not be bought with things. I was far too cerebral. I needed repentance. I wanted blood. Until I heard some sort of acceptance of guilt, I was simply going to tolerate them. Could I love them? With what?

> *"With my love. Remember Philippians 4:13, 'I can do all things through Christ who strengthens me.' I am the Vine, you are the branch; to produce the fruit of the Spirit you must allow me to flow through you. Without Me you will break off and die. Now tell me, is your need for revenge worth that? What about all the plans The Father has for you? What about your son? Is this what you want to teach him? Hate? Anger?"*

I pleaded for Jesus to supernaturally set me free. He heard me, day in, day out, but He was not going to pry my fingers open. He waited patiently until one day I asked Him and meant it. I was ready to open my hands and let go. I could no longer blame the mother and daughter-in-law syndrome. I could no longer lead Bible studies in my home and skirt around the issue of love. Reading 1 Corinthians 13 was like having little daggers jabbing me.

> *"Love...does not seek its own...is not provoked...does not take into account a wrong suffered...bears all things...endures all things...." 1 Corinthians 13:5 & 7.*

It was most difficult for me to accept that I may never hear the human words I felt would heal me. I had to trust that in Jesus' stripes I would be healed. My father had always said, "Reconciliation began with the relationship between God and man, then man to man." I had to abide in God, then He would abide in me, and I would bear much fruit, but without Him, I could do nothing. I could not love my fellow human beings. I would cease to be productive and become instead a clanging cymbal. I wanted to be a sweet, sweet sound in His ears, not a noisy gong. I wanted to love.

It was not long after that that I remember feeling the strangest feeling. Ken and I had taken Jordan out for a walk when I spotted a woman who looked just like Ken's mother. I almost wished it was her! I actually wanted to see my mother-in-law! I checked inside my heart for the hate I had cherished so closely before and it was gone.

Ken almost fell over when I told him that I actually had no more bitterness for his parents. I had forgiven them, because certainly I had been forgiven much and would undoubtedly be forgiven much more in the future. I could put the past behind me. I could move forward again. I could be a real donkey for Jesus now, knowing that as long as I abided in Him, He would always abide in me with the Spirit of truth and real Christian love.

In a world where people were dying to see Jesus I could once again transport the "Good News" of His miraculous healing power in a vessel that was worthy of it, redeemed by that precious blood, set free to a love that is blind. I could lift up a life that reflected the light of God's love, and that would draw all men and women, boys and girls to Himself and to each other in one big, beautiful flame. All glory to The Father of our Lord and Saviour Jesus Christ!

Chapter 11

Who Will Save the Children?

O ne of my favourite songs is by Carman, and it is in the form of a dialogue between God and his child. God speaks and says;

> *"Child, don't look behind you.*
> *Discouragement is all you'll find.*
> *Don't watch the waves that roll the sea,*
> *but just focus your eyes on Me,*
> *and I will make you strong and then*
> *your shattered courage I will mend.*
> *And if you fall and should get hurt,*
> *remember these eternal words -*
> *Fear not my child, I'm with you always.*
> *I feel every pain and every tear I see.*
> *Fear not my child, I'm with you always,*
> *I know how to care for what belongs to me."*

Those are the sweetest words in my ear. God knows how to care for what belongs to Him. I belong to Him. Every volatile molecule in me belongs to God. My time. My energy. My thoughts. My desires. My devotion. My husband. My child...

To me, motherhood has got to be the most profound relationship in the world. It has been proven that the strongest human instinct is not self-preservation, as commonly thought, but the maternal instinct. There's something about carrying life inside of you, and the subsequent process of childbirth that makes a woman want to kill for her child, even die for it. Yet who would have known that in the twentieth century we would witness the emergence of women serial killers? What has gone so wrong in our societies, that women, the life-bringers, can turn around and kill their own children?

As I have listened to women in America and counseled with them, it somehow does not surprise me that women have gone so wrong. Little girls all across America are being abused repeatedly, sexually, emotionally and psychologically by their fathers, or stepfathers, or related males. The very men who are supposed to be building up those little girls' confidences are the very ones who are destroying them with their own sick lusts. Those little girls are growing up sick, confused, guilty, feeling worthless, and this is made worse by their mothers' refusal to believe them or do anything to help them. When they become mothers, they, too, stand quietly by as their daughters are molested by the men in their lives, or worse, they become the abusers. They take their anger and shame out on the children.

The story of little Adam, who by the age of five had had every bone in his little body broken by his mother, affected me in an extraordinary way. Adam never got to see his sixth birthday. I wept with grief for Adam. I wept, and wept, and wept for the pain he had had to experience throughout his short life. I wanted to wrap him tightly in my arms and love all that pain away. But it was too late for little Adam, his potential had been snuffed out by his own mother.

The life and death of little Adam would not have devastated me to the extent that it did, had I not been a mother myself. I would not have fully appreciated the preciousness of children, and the importance of a mother in creating their joyfulness.

Before I became a mother, I had actually bought into the myth of the superwoman: simultaneously superwife, supermother, super successful career person. Conflicting reports on the welfare of children brought up in the day-care system helped keep me in denial about the toll a career would have on my children, or my marriage.

The road to motherhood led me back to the basics. Back to the things that really matter: a faith in God, a loving and supportive partnership in marriage, and the raising of happy, healthy children. Careers are important, too, for we must have creative ways to express ourselves, but I was to learn that in God's economy everything had its season. The Proverbs 31 woman did not happen overnight, and she did not do everything at the same time. God had perfect timing. My job was to simply trust God and allow Him to move me in the way He had planned for me. That, as you probably know, was easier said than done.

The day I found out I was pregnant I fell to the floor and cried. For the nights that followed I knelt in our dark living room begging the Lord to take 'it' away. I felt Ken and I had not been given enough time alone together, and I still had so much to do to get my career off the ground. Before that shock had worn off, Ken and I were hit with another one. My Ob/Gyn told me I was a C-section candidate. I was too narrow to deliver a baby naturally. Me, the woman who hated hospitals with a passion was now destined to be taken to one and cut open to deliver this baby! There had to be another option.

To top it off, the costs of delivering a baby by C-section in an American hospital (where a two dollar bottle of aspirin can cost more than fifty dollars) were outrageous, and my transfer onto Ken's insurance had not yet kicked in. Where were we going to get that kind of money so soon after the wedding? The doctor seemed unsympathetic. "Natural childbirth will be too dangerous for you," she insisted.

I couldn't accept that, not while there was still a God in heaven. Already suspicious of the medical profession in America, my doctor did nothing to assuage my fears. During the couple of months I went to her for prenatal care she never once met Ken, or even inquired about him, even though he went with me on every visit. Her 'concern' centered around how much weight I had gained, but only as a matter of routine. No inquires were ever made of what I was eating, and no suggestions were offered. I found out that doctors were not trained in nutrition, so she wasn't able to offer me the information I needed.

Yet after each visit I came out seventy dollars poorer, and for what? For the privilege of waiting in her waiting room for half an hour, and a minute of her time answering a few precautionary questions? And perhaps a urine test, for which I had to pay extra and never seemed to get the results. And what did I have to look forward to at the end? To be cut open, most probably out of fear of a malpractice suit rather than the fact that I couldn't deliver the child naturally. Over a third of all C-sections performed on women in America were unnecessary.

Ken and I went before the Lord in prayer and sought in His Word for guidance. "Those who wait upon the Lord..." Sure enough, true to His promise of answering His children's prayers, the Lord brought a woman into our life who was about to deliver her third child at home, naturally, with a midwife. Yes! This was our answer. "...will gain new strength;" I got the name of her mid-wife and I called immediately. "...they will mount up with wings like eagles..." Isaiah 40:31. We both liked her instantly. We'd like to think it was mutual.

From the very beginning she made Ken an integral part of the equation. She was committed to making 'our' pregnancy the beautiful bonding experience God had intended it to be. Through her I began to see the child as the expression of our love, a gift God had chosen to bestow upon us to bless us, not as an inconvenient interruption in our lives. Now we had found the missing link, God's chosen care provider for us—a midwife, just like in the Bible. Talk about going back to the basics—a home-birth. It was radical, but it felt very right.

Joan took extensive precautionary tests and filled out a questionnaire on my history and habits that was so comprehensive it was embarrassing at times. She was as thorough as the doctor had been unthorough. She insisted on seeing me regularly for a full hour at a time, and went as far as working out a menu for me, writing down the items I was to buy and where to buy them! Sugar was out, refined or artificial anything was out, and intake was regularly increased to accommodate the growing child.

Meanwhile, Ken was commissioned to keep praying that God would provide safe passageway for the child, for I was, indeed, narrow, especially for the size of baby I was carrying. Joan gave us Isaiah 66:9 to hang on to. "Shall I bring to the point of birth and not give delivery?" says the LORD. "Or shall I who gives delivery shut the womb?" says your God.

Perhaps what stood out the most in Joan was her love for children and her passion to bring them into the world in the most joyous, peaceful way possible. This involved keeping the mother healthy and happy, and the family situation into which the child would come, loving and united in Christ.

Midway through the pregnancy, I had to have an ultrasound to make sure I wasn't carrying twins. Ken and I sighed with relief when Joan told us it was just one long baby. Having a hospital back-up was a matter of routine, and we promised Joan that if at any point during the delivery she said, "We're going to the hospital," we were to do exactly as she said. She would still deliver the baby, but with hospital support.

The weekly childbirth classes she gave for all her pregnant couples was a great experience; we enjoyed the different people. I particularly found great solace in being with other women who were also going through the ballooning experience. One thing we didn't necessarily like was the homework, but it was mandatory. The decision to have a home-birth was a serious one, there was much to learn. In case of the rare emergency (i.e., the baby wants out and Joan is caught in traffic, or stopped for speeding), Ken needed to be able to deliver the baby and keep mother and child comfortable until professional help arrived.

After a wonderful prenatal experience, Jordan Alexander was brought into the world at home, naturally, with Ken and my sister present, and two midwives I trusted fully (Joan and her good friend and colleague, Roberta) guiding and helping me. I had three brothers pacing out in the living room, and when things got too intense, one would retreat out to his car to call his co-workers at the office and give them an animated blow-by-blow account of the delivery, "She's having the baby right now as we speak."

Later, in the comfort of my bedroom, we were all able to talk to my mother on a speaker phone (she was stuck in London with visa problems), and tell her that her grandson had arrived safely into the world and both mother and child were doing just fine. Now I know why God kept my mother stranded in London, she would have gone nuts. My brothers were still trying to come to grips with the whole experience. They had been closer to the action than they had ever hoped to be. Joan had called them in to see the baby within minutes of its birth. God had been most faithful.

"I know how to care for what belongs to me."

Ken and I had decided to trust the word of God over the word of a doctor. We believed there were legitimate needs for doctors, but didn't feel this was one of them. We kept in constant prayer so we would not listen to the voices of 'reason and knowledge' that tried to persuade us into a hospital birth. It was a wimpy Christians need not apply' kind of adventure, but I felt sincerely that I did not need to go to the hospital; hospitals were for sick people, I was not sick. I was just having a baby—the most natural and wondrous of all female functions. I could do that at home. If my grandmother could do it all alone out in the bushes of Africa while on a hunting trip with my grandfather, then I certainly could do it under the careful and prayerful assistance of God's chosen messengers. Not one, but two.

Everything about the experience was perfect (a few scares were thrown in for good measure, and we won't talk about the forty-three pounds, the swollen ankles, or the pain); the important thing was that Jordan did not have to come into the world in a noisy, unnaturally bright environment. He was not pulled out of my stomach by a pair of foreign hands belonging to an 'anxious to get back onto the golf course' doctor wielding steel forceps. He was not drowsy from drugs injected into my body to make it easier for me. His heel was not pricked prematurely. He was not carted off and put in a nursery. He did not have to suffer a car ride home in an oversize car seat. And...I didn't end up with a stomach full of stitches.

When Jordan was ready he found his way out. Joan welcomed him into the world by name, wiped him gently and then placed him on my chest. Within seconds of his birth we were skin to skin, looking at each other, his eyes fully open and alert. At that moment, this warrior woman fell desperately in love with a nine pound bundle of precious, beautiful, healthy baby boy. It was an overwhelming feeling.

Many of my heroines are strong leaders and invariably all these strong warrior types became softer after childbirth. Their aggressive instincts were replaced with maternal love. They suddenly saw their male opponents as some woman's child who should be loved and nurtured—not tortured and destroyed. I had joined the ranks of those doting, overprotective human beings, I became a mother. I had made the decision to have my heart walking around outside my body forever. And it was as a mother that I now had to make choices for my life, particularly in the area of my career?

Before Jordan's birth, I had interviewed with several caregivers for I fully intended to go back to work. I had just spent seven years of valuable career time waiting on the Lord, and now that I had a green card I was ready to test my wings in the marketplace. To stay at home and care for Jordan would cost me another four to five years; I'd be ancient by then. I'd never catch up with my contemporaries. Besides, wasn't it the '90s thing to do? All this was while Jordan was still faceless.

The minute we looked into that helpless little face, we both knew I was the only one qualified for the job of caring for him. I provided the food that would give him optimum nourishment during his first two years, so I had to stay close. The term 'dairy queen' took on a whole new meaning. Ken and I made the choice to return to the basics. We decided to scrimp and get by on one salary, live in a one bedroom apartment, shelve a car in order to give our child his mother as his primary care-provider.

We had absolute faith that God would provide and take care of us because this was His choice for Jordan. It was also His choice for me; it gave me a chance to experiment with my writing (and cooking), and to grow in wifehood and motherhood. It was also God's choice for Ken, because Ken thrived on being the sole provider for his family. His devotion to us was written all over his face. Indeed, he was just like my father.

There was a time I used to bristle whenever I read 1 Timothy 2:15, "But women shall be preserved through the bearing of children if they continue in faith and love and sanctity with self-restraint," particularly since it came after several verses in which Paul seemed to bash women, blaming them for the fall through Eve. However, now I feel preserved. Motherhood has rounded me out as a person, and I say unequivocally that these have been the best years of my life. I have never experienced so much love, so much joy, so much peace as I have caring for that little one, watching him grow, and sharing all these experiences with the man God has so greatly gifted me with, enjoying his love, and watching him delight in his son. I know what it feels like for my cup to 'runneth over'. These have been the dividends I have reaped for going back to the basics and making God's choices my choices by putting my family before my career.

Recently, I looked through Jordan's earlier pictures and I shuddered to think of all the precious moments I would have missed had I insisted on following my own sorry agenda, or an agenda prescribed by society. I had nothing to prove by going into the work force during the time my child needed me most—I could give birth...what more did I have to prove? Men could never survive the experience. What was it about the rat race anyway, that would have made it worth the loss of all those memories?

I thank God for each woman who has chosen to tighten her budget in order to stay home and raise her children, and each man who has chosen to take on the responsibility of supporting his family, thus allowing his wife to be all she was meant to be, and raise the children she was meant to raise. I applaud the fathers who have chosen to stay at home and raise their children in the cases where it is best that the woman be the breadwinner. I pray that God revives more hearts towards home.

If it is indeed true that the hand that rocks the cradle rules the world, then it is no wonder our societies are so off kilter. More and more the hands that are rocking the cradles have grown up with a warped sense of what a family is, and with little responsibility to it. The intact two-parent family has fallen on hard times in the western world. There are fewer and fewer models around. Indeed the very institution of marriage itself is being denigrated more than it is being lifted up. Yet how can you blame people for repeating what they saw?

Many people, in calling for other people to take responsibility for their lives, forget that what has been put into a person is what comes out. In a godless society, how do we know what a godly marriage is like, if it isn't modeled for us? How can we make godly decisions when in many cases our parents didn't even teach us about God? We must be taught, otherwise we go from one marriage to another trying to make it work. Ken and I don't know how to be dysfunctional, it wasn't modeled for us. We only know how to care and support each other just as our parents supported and cared for each other. That is what we saw, that is what we learned. Now we must model it and teach our son.

If we are to resurrect the status of marriage and the family in our societies, we must first balance the hand that rocks the cradle. My older brother, Edward, a fellow contemplative, believes that the state of the collective world of women in each respective nation will determine the health and material welfare of all the peoples of that society. He suggests that instead of looking at life only through masculine eyes and minds, as has been the case up to now, a new feminine perspective with its unique sensitivity must be included in formulating the future direction of society.

However, women cannot live without men, and men cannot live without women. The human race depends on both. Each needs the other. It was a man who shaped the woman in me. My father. It is a man who now brings out the woman in me, my husband. These are the most critical relationships in a woman's life. If your father shaped you to be a pillar of society, then you will be a pillar of society and your children and husband will rise and call you blessed. If he shaped you to be a punching bag, then you will mostly likely marry a man who will treat you like a punching bag, and your children will rise and call you cursed.

Who can understand why so many men have gone so wrong in our societies? Who can understand why a man beats his wife and abuses his children? Over fifty percent of all the women killed in America in any given year are killed by their husbands. Over two hundred thousand children a year in America are sexually abused within the home. We can cry with the Psalmist, "Help, Lord, for the godly are no more; the faithful have vanished from among men." Psalm 12:1. This is the same cry for the church of the 1990s.

Who can understand why so many Christian men in America have no desire or interest in the things of God? If the Christian man is the conduit through which his family receives protection and guidance from the Lord, then families across this nation are not receiving that protection and guidance. America is a country crumbling from the inside. Inside homes all across this nation lights big and small are being snuffed out systematically. The lack of God's presence is making home a very dangerous place for many Americans. The devil is destroying everything in sight; the primary targets—our marriages and our children.

This country needs help. It has gone as far as I care to see it go because I am a mother. The most precious gift given to a woman by God is that of new life, so why are so many of our children hurting so desperately? I weep for the children of America. Mind you, I am acutely aware of the physical suffering of 'my children' in Africa and it's only a matter of time before the Lord sends me back to fight for them, but meanwhile my many years in this country have shown me that emotional and spiritual pain are perhaps the most devastating.

I have witnessed first hand the mass human suffering of the children of this 'great' nation, and it breaks my heart. They are assaulted on every front. Each year over a million and a half meet the grim reaper before they can even make it out of the womb. Those that make it out are liable to come out with an addiction or two, or three; many face lifelong disorders, some have fatal diseases. Those that are unwanted are thrown into a foster care system that destroys whatever bit of self-esteem they may have been able to salvage. If that doesn't get them, then the pressure cooker of junior high will. The devil is on a rampage so deadly and so heinous that all that's left to do is echo the sentiment, "America, you're too young to die."

So where is the hope? Where can we go to find the answers? Jesus Christ. It is now time for women to reclaim their homes and take back their families for Christ. It is time to determine that loving, nurturing and protecting our children is our number one priority as mothers. We are the teachers and, in the absence of significant male involvement, we must also take on the responsibility of providing for them and guiding them. In cases where abuse is present, we must take the responsibility to pack up those bags and take our children to a safe place. We can no longer stand quietly by and watch the souls of our children being trashed every day and stripped of their dignity. Responsibility must become our new buzz word. Living examined lives, accountable to God, being the kind of wives and mothers He would have us to be. Anything else is not worth living.

In order to live godly lives, women must first be healed. Many have grown up repeatedly being told through word and deed that they are nothing, and that they will never amount to anything, they will never fly. On top of that, their God-given gifts have been stolen or defiled, many have been left with only broken wings and distant dreams. We must not pass this legacy on to the cradle. There is healing in the name of Jesus. Let us be the ones who stop the madness, who stop the cycle of abuse, drugs and crime.

The stolen dreams, the years eaten by the locusts, the unloved heart, all these can and must find healing in the name of Jesus. I agree with my brother that it will be through the influence and lives of the women of the household of God that true and lasting healing to the wider world of women and children, and even men, can occur. For the blind cannot lead us out of darkness; those with eyes that see and with the light of Christ must take on that responsibility. "It is imperative," he says, "that a spiritually grounded, Christian feminine dimension and agenda must be brought to bear in the re-creation of our societies and the crafting of a new paradigm for the future."

Indeed, we are witnessing the possibilities, for while male pastors have been seeking status and power, a silent revolution has been going on as women pastors lead their congregations into the healing of damaged emotions, broken families and violent communities. Women evangelists are breathing new life into our congregations and inspiring us with new visions. This is only a beginning, there is still so much to do.

This is a call to women, those who call themselves by His name; it's time for God's Iron Ladies. No more wimpy mothering. It's time for us as our Father's Daughters to take advantage of all the love our Father in Heaven is waiting to lavish upon us. We must recapture the vision of being Daddy's girl with all the unconditional acceptance that that relationship brings when it is experienced in all its purity and strength. Only then will we be able to unleash some of that love on the world we influence, beginning with our families.

There is a line in a popular song that goes, "How long will it take to start all over?" How long will it take to return to the basics and make the family our first responsibility? How long will it take for Christian women to stop cowering in defense-mode and start marching in offense-mode, on the front lines to recapture our children? How long will it take to realize we've wasted so much time already? So what if the world ridicules the traditional family structure as outdated? Why should they rain on our parade? They only mock it because they are so depraved and so unhappy.

I get great satisfaction in seeing the mockers of Dan Quayle now publicly admitting that there is no social program invented by man that can replace the two-parent family in developing happy, balanced individuals. This was common sense then, it's still common sense today. To deny this is to reap destructive and immoral behaviour as evidenced in American society today. Broken lives from broken homes are strewn from coast to coast. This is a nation of broken people, with the church no less a victim.

The increasing incidence of divorce, and the rise of out-of-wedlock promiscuity, have left a large number of Christian women alone to parent their children. Here it is not whether to be or not to be a superwoman, there is no choice. One person has to be mother, father, provider, playmate, teacher, counselor, friend, disciplinarian, all at the same time. I take off my hat to single mothers. I don't know how they do it.

Yet, even though many have risen to the challenge and are raising good children, it was never God's intention that children go to bed every night without a father present in the home. It was never God's intention that one person shoulder all the responsibilities of a household. It was never God's intention that women work while other people raise their small children. Children brought up under these circumstances are more prone to outside influences and destructive behaviours than those raised with both parents present and positively involved.

God has an infinitely better plan for each one of us, and for our families, but first we must reconcile with Him. We must live in right relationship with Him. We must learn to trust Him as our Father. Only when we learn to think of Him as "Daddy" will we be able to think of ourselves as precious and loved beyond compare. Only then will we experience our true beauty and joy. Otherwise we will be doomed to cultural Christianity that has studied God into a formula, instead of studying God to seek His heart, to fall in love with Him, a real person, a real relationship.

This is the relationship that must be restored if women are to play a part in God's vision to restore families and save the children of this great nation. We cannot save our children from drowning if we are treading water ourselves. We must take responsibility for our own healing; then, whole ourselves, we will lead this nation into wholeness.

We must ask ourselves, "If not us, then who? If not now, then when?" If we accept our responsibility to the future generation, then once again, the open, infectious laughter of little children at play will be heard and nurtured in our homes and in our communities. Let us positively exercise our power of mother-love on our children's wounds. It is the strongest tonic known to mankind. They are depending on us, there is no one else who will stand in the gap for them, so let's just do it.

Chapter 12

When Eagles Soar

Uncommon love and uncommon obedience beget radical servanthood. That's what characterizes an eagle that soars. Before the Lord sends an eagle out of the nest to soar He must first prepare her and teach her how to fly. He must first put her through His personal school of evangelism and this He does in the church. The Lord tests our love and faith within the church family first. No eagle was ever sent out into the world to love the unsaved before she learned how to love and serve God's people. There is no way we can love strangers if we do not love our brothers and sisters in the Lord. It is also impossible to survive in battle alone without the support of a church family.

At the time Ken and I got married in 1988, our church encouraged newly married couples to take a year off from ministry to concentrate on each other and their marriage. It was a good idea, and most couples did so gladly, but I did not feel the need to do so, so I continued my fight for the souls of the college group during that first year and throughout my pregnancy. I remember being asked to give the message when I was too pregnant to stand for more than five minutes, so they let me sit to speak to them.

I found that God has an uncanny way of teaching you the lesson after you have gone through the experience. I guess that's what faith is all about. Doing away with all claims to security, privilege, position and status, and calling into being a whole new order of thought—freely accepted servanthood. My journey in pursuit of radical servanthood was painful. I do not necessarily want to relive it, but again the freedom I now experience warrants my recounting my lows as well as my ups.

I had a hero in the Bible; I had fallen in love with the greatest of all servants, Moses. Moses was a man who managed to find his way into many religions of the world as a true prophet of God. Why? My opinion is that it was because of his humility. Moses is reported to have been the humblest man on earth. His obedience to God was unparalleled, and God spoke to him face to face. Moses dared to leave all behind, to come, take off his shoes and walk onto holy ground before the Almighty God of Heaven and earth; to listen to what He had to say to him and the people of Israel. What he lacked in character and confidence Moses made up for in commitment.

God's servant Moses. I liked the sound of that. God's servant Victoria. What type of faith did it take to see God face to face? Was this call only for a very select few? In Matthew 5:8 it promised that all who were pure in heart were blessed and would see God. Would I ever allow Jesus to purify my heart enough to see God? I certainly wanted to be one of the select.

I was learning to accept both the good and the bad of my mission. I was finally able to admit that I was a missionary-of-sorts to America. We must understand that towards the end of the eighties, the concept of a self-supporting African being a missionary to America was still as foreign as Uganda supplying oil to the Middle East. The myth was that missionaries were sent by churches and organizations from rich countries. Africa was too poor to offer America anything. Now the Lord was ready to change all of that, beginning in my mind and heart.

The Holy Spirit was the Commander in Chief of the Missionary Enterprise and His requirements had nothing to do with material wealth and everything to do with heart wealth. Certainly the church in Africa had infinitely more flavour and evangelistic zeal than the joyless churches in America where they had managed to materialize the spiritual. Sin was only sin if you could see it (woe to the alcoholic and substance abuser). Americans needed to experience the spiritual. They desperately needed to know that the basis of life was, after all, spiritual—something Africans took for granted, for to them there was no separation of the sacred and the secular. Life was religion and religion was life.

The downside of my mission was that the message was tougher than most Americans were willing to take. I had an uphill fight on my hands, against the flow all the way. Sometimes I wondered whether revival would ever come to America. The hearts of the people seemed too calloused, too proud, too self-sufficient. I sometimes had to wonder whether they were reading from the same Bible I was. Somehow the word of God was not making it to the brain center. I kept my heart turned to the Lord.

Your people, Lord, I don't know about them. They just want their ears tickled. We aren't getting through. Maybe it is time to go back home. They don't want me here any more than I want to be here. Besides, Africa needs me more now than ever.

> *"Just trust me. Besides, your being here is not for their sake as much as it is for yours. You must learn to love this country, otherwise we could be here a while."*

I was afraid of that. I had to learn to love this country, otherwise I wouldn't get to see mine for a while. This was going to be a long stop because I didn't know how to begin to love America. I didn't even know how to let Jesus love it through me. Yet now the most important person in my physical world was American and I had to find something to love about his country. I enjoyed the comfort and convenience of this wealthy nation, but I was unhappy with the Christians. They were so wimpy I found no genuine fellowship among them. I longed for the spontaneous joy of the African fellowship.

> *"I want you to raise up an army of eagles for me. God is preparing the way for a mighty worldwide revival. Wake them up."*

My Lord Jesus, how was I going to make these young people understand that while this culture seemed to worship their youth, it was only to exploit it and eventually destroy it? How could I make them see that barring premature death, they, too, would eventually grow old? And then what? They were making decisions with no forethought to the spiritual consequences. How could I show them that the American dream was a trap for eagles?

That look came upon Jesus' face again. The spotlight was turned on me. I braced myself, because I was most probably about to find out something ugly about myself.

> *"Before we worry about that, we have to tone you down. You can't operate your blowtorch on high all the time. You must get acquainted with some of the gentler levels. You'll find they'll respond to the message better when it is first of all in love, and you'll bring a sweeter sacrifice to the Lord."*

Graciousness again. My lack of it. Out of frustration with the college group, I distanced myself using Jordan as my excuse, but I kept in touch through the young women I discipled weekly in my home. I had a game plan. I figured that if I set these lives on fire, they would head back into the group and set it ablaze. So, I danced the truth before them, and sang the love of God. I took the truth from their abstract propositions and set it in exciting human drama. I challenged them to a faith that was not only expressed, but also demonstrated. I kept trying to push them out of the nest.

It wasn't working. As soon as they attempted to seek changes in the main group, they would be squelched by the powers that be and they would back off. Eventually they wandered off into some other less threatening, more convenient ministry, and this usually distanced them from me and my unrelenting demand for excellence. They would drop out of the group and new, daring ones would step in and the cycle would begin again.

Every three months or so, I would be invited back to give the Sunday morning message to the group. Jesus wanted me to teach them about passion. So, on passion I spoke... passionately, and they would catch it for that day, and possibly the next, but it was all just surfacey emotionalism, the seeds never took root. When the pedal hit the metal, their rubber hit the road in the opposite direction, going with the flow. A few lone eagles stuck with me until Jesus felt they were ready and sent them on their own missions, but they were too few and far between for me. The army was not happening as fast as I had hoped.

Jesus gave me vision after vision. I started a young African women's fellowship, and at first we seemed to be doing well, we had a group of twelve. Then commitments started to fall through, and disunity among members finally led the group to dissolve. I couldn't compete with the pen, it asked for little responsibility and no accountability. Jesus asked for excellence and accountability to Him in all things.

The kind of commitment I was asking for, both in the African and American groups I was leading, was not there for every excuse imaginable. I heard them all. A generation raised on MTV was looking for a performer, not a prophet; that was considered B.C., these were the nineties. I was trying to teach them, they preferred to be tickled. I offered them the Spirit, they were more interested in the flesh.

At a point of real frustration, with my fingers dancing dangerously close to my DELETE button, I asked Jesus why He didn't just will them to love Him? After all Philippians 2:13 said, "...He was the one who was at work in them, both to will and to work for His good pleasure."

> **"The operative words being 'in them.' I am not in them. They have been given the will, but they have chosen to ignore the promptings, much like you, my friend, when you ignore the oil light in your car."**

Boy. What happened to parables? Stories about other people who had problems. The operative word here being 'other.'

> **"Don't give up, there will be a remnant who will take the time to listen, and to reason out their faith into action. Have a little patience."**

That was like appealing to my little finger to hang on to a bowling ball by itself. It was time to learn that I was only as strong as my weakest link, and patience headed that list. Jesus was beginning to teach me how to adjust the temperature gauge on my blowtorch by first attacking my attitude. It was tedious, time-consuming, impatience-consuming work, for it was my impatience that kept it on red-hot all the time. I hadn't wanted to be bothered to stop and care for the individual inside the little eaglet, I just wanted them to fly. I wanted them to start 'the revival.' The one that would rock the world.

As I slowed down and started really listening, really feeling their pain, I discovered that the majority of these young people had absolutely no idea what it was to love God. To simply, naturally love God. So many were caught up in the fog of family dysfunction that they couldn't quite grasp the concept of an everloving, gracious God. Because of that, Christianity was a task, a chore they failed at miserably. Without heart-to-heart with God they had nothing, and the sad fact was that they couldn't see it. I was never quite sure if the leadership did either. The concentration was still on knowing more about God than on loving Him.

Oh, they were ready to defend and justify their commitments, but unfortunately for them, the presence of, or lack of this love for God was very easy to detect. I could see when God's love was manifested in a person's heart because it produced fruit, and the first fruit was joy. Pure and simple joy. A concept so obvious you'd have to pay someone to confuse it for you. This joy of the Lord made you fall in love with His people and this led to automatic service to them. A follower of Jesus was always in service with the 'strength of the Lord'—JOY.

I would look into the eyes of these brave young soldiers and hope and pray for joy. This was their greatest weapon, and they were fighting the spiritual forces without it. This was not the road to revival. This was a sure-fire formula for defeat. Occasionally, I would see glimmers of joy, but even these were simply moments of happiness because things were going well for them. Most often life was a struggle and I was learning to hurt with them instead of forcing them to do something they were ill-equipped and ill-prepared for. Jesus was teaching me to love each and every one that He placed in my care.

So many times I felt so helpless all I could do was put my arm around them. I wanted so desperately to see them fly high above it all, smiling from the inside out. I had been spoiled by the infectious joy I saw in the young Christians in Uganda when I spent four weeks there in 1986 filming the documentary. I knew that the same Jesus who put those smiles in the African heart could put those same smiles in the American heart. I soon became impatient to see Him do it, and the challenge began to take on a harder edge than necessary.

Then a bombshell fell. Our pastor, the reason I was at that church, felt a calling to take on a ministry elsewhere. I was shattered. I adored him. I had looked at him as a sort of father figure. The only reason I believed in the church was because I believed in him. I knew his heart, and it was pure. I believed he was going up the mountain and receiving the word for us, but I also knew the frustrations he was encountering in getting the word through to the people. At first I couldn't bring myself to believe the words that had come out of his mouth. He was leaving! He couldn't. We had a mission here to bring revival to this church. Every time I saw him I wanted to cry, and then he was gone. Who would believe in me now? Who could I trust to be in my corner?

Jesus pulled me aside. It was time to abide. Time to chill out and smell the roses. Jesus and I strolled by the still waters, and sat a while in the green pastures. The Christian movement would not die if I went into seclusion for a while, it would probably benefit. I enrolled in a writing class and concentrated on writing a screenplay. For two years I watched from the sidelines as the church went through the trauma of finding a new leader. Ironically, the college group was also going through a transition as it, too, lost its pastor and membership declined.

Then it was show time again. I was asked to speak to the college group. By now we had new pastors for both the church and the college group.

> **"I want you to start a movement. This time, instead of just speaking to them and then running off, I want you to call the eagles in the group to start a movement to set this nation back on course."**

A movement? I thought we were in this for revival? You know, the supernatural flow of energy that would fall upon us and then just roll off of us and suffuse the nation. A movement sounded like a lot of tedious work, a lot of organizing, and I was not particularly into organizations. I quite preferred the independent career. Jump in, jump-start them, jump out and leave the consequences to Jesus.

> **"We have to start a grassroots movement among the youth, church to church across the nation, then the world."**

I suddenly heard the words, my father's voice straining to stay under control. I had just returned from a trip into Uganda with an Australian couple that had met with my wrath. I tried to reason with my father, to make him understand why I had lost my temper. After all, at one stop they had arranged for me to sleep in a mosquito-infested room while they slept in a comfortable room. What made them so special? This time they had messed with the wrong African. The second-class citizen bit didn't fly with me.

The words had come out of his mouth slowly and deliberately, "You have a rare combination of passion and anger—the kind that begins movements—the kind that can lead this vision into the twenty-first century, but not before you do something about that temper!" Somehow the word 'movement' had always seemed reserved for the Martin Luther Kings, the Malcolm X's, people who could control their anger under severe pressure. Did this call mean I had learned to control my temper?

"I sought the Lord, and He answered me, and delivered me from all my fears." Psalm 34:4.

"I will instruct you and teach you in the way which you should go; I will counsel you with My eye upon you." Psalm 32:8.

"For God has not given me a spirit of timidity, but of power and love and discipline." 2 Timothy 1:7.

So it happened that I stood up before a group of over one hundred college students and made a call to those who were tired of living a wimpy Christianity to join me in starting a movement—LIFE-BRINGERS—a radical movement of God to reclaim the lost generation. I received just over twenty responses. These, I felt, were Jesus' chosen eaglets. I would teach them how to fly and together we would go and fish out their contemporaries caught in the pits of hell. I was excited. I was soaring.

For the next four months I was consumed by LIFE-BRINGERS, dragging Ken and Jordan into it with me. I soon found out that my blowtorch was never on the right temperature. I was so sure these were all eagle material that I was shocked by all the sensitivity I encountered. I tried to be responsive and was continually turning my temperature down to accommodate them, but eventually I reached the lowest temperature on my torch, and soon the numbers began to dwindle until it wasn't worth my time anymore. I wiped my feet.

It had all been one big flesh dance. Meeting once a week was too much. I wasn't loving enough. I expected too much from them. Too much homework. I wasn't as excited over their birthdays as I was expected to be. LIFE-BRINGERS was getting in the way of their social lives. I was too self-righteous. I was too critical of some of the decisions made by the powers that be. In short, they weren't ready (willing or able) to fly. I could not make them understand that this was a training opportunity, not a ministry unto itself. When they failed to catch a vision for their lives, the passion they had first come into the group with perished and they with it.

It was over. The movement had not happened, but I had learned the most fascinating lessons of my life, learning more of the true meaning of Christlike love and humility. Instead of the movement being a failure as many thought, it had been the road to victory. It had been hard, and I had shed more tears than I care to admit to, but through LIFE-BRINGERS doors opened up to ministries outside of the church. I got a chance to teach at a women's shelter over a period of several months. I also joined hands with other eagles in an inner-city ministry that led to a very rewarding prison ministry. The mission was accomplished.

Chapter 13

Where Have All the Heroes Gone?

"Why are we in such a mess?
Where are the heroes now,
when we need them so desperately?
Who will step out from the crowd
and be strong enough to lead?
Who will teach the children, who will show them how?
Oh, I'm asking you, where are the heroes now?"

Steve Camp, FIRE AND ICE

"Remember those who led you, who spoke the word of God to you; and considering the result of their conduct, imitate their faith." Hebrews 13:7.

A few years ago I wrote in my journal; "It would be tragic if, with such a role model as my father, I never imitated his faith. I have more respect for him as a man of God than any other human being I've ever known or met. His was a special faith, and it will continue to challenge me for the rest of my life."

The year I worked on the documentary of my father's life and ministry was like an intensive one-year course on understanding John Wilson, the man and the evangelist. My father was great at taping his sermons with a small cassette recorder, so after his death I rounded up as many tapes as I could and listened to each one very carefully. I read through file after file of his work and looked at hundreds of photos. I reread all his letters to me. I read his journals, his message outlines, his correspondence. I recorded people's testimonies about him. I watched all his interviews, reviewed home movies. Out of all that research, I came to know more about my father than I did when he was alive, and I admired everything I found out about him. I was again intrigued by his ability to articulate the gospel so simply and beautifully that it was irresistible even to those who were running away from it. I told myself that if I could be even twenty percent of John Wilson, I'd make it in life

My father's faith and love were extraordinary gifts given to him by the Lord, gifts that he multiplied by being tuned to the Master's tuning fork every minute of every day. The objective of his life's game plan was to get as close to Jesus as possible. The winner, in his eyes, was the one who got the closest to Jesus. In my lifetime, the winner was John Wilson. That's why my father was, and will always be, my greatest earthly hero. It is his life that I seek to model myself after. I want to be the winner of my generation, following in his footsteps. Pure, unadulterated faith. As close to the flame as humanly possible. To be one with Christ in thought, word and deed; not merely playing with His love, but soaked in it to the bone.

My father had the stature of a true worshiper of Jesus Christ. He was a hero to the thousands of people he reached out and touched in his lifetime. A look into his gentle brown eyes always warmed the spirit. For him to be like Jesus was to be in the business of warming spirits, of bringing healing and hope to broken hearts, and food and clothing to hungry and naked bodies. Like Jesus, he was interested in the whole person and both his/her immediate and future needs.

Where have all the heroes gone? What a lament is going on in every sector of our societies across the globe, but most pitifully in our homes where the true heroes should be and aren't. Not long ago I conducted an informal survey among my siblings and all of us, bar none, said our Dad was our greatest hero "in a class all by himself." As I watch my own little in-house eaglet prancing about to Carmen's song "Revival in the Land" (a.k.a. "Jesus gets the bad guys") and singing in a high voice, "Revival is coming to the land," I am struck poignantly about this issue of parents as heroes. I love it when children, especially black children, say proudly that their Dad and Mum are their heroes—and not an athlete or entertainer.

When Jordan comes home from preschool (where he goes part-time to knock heads with people of like mind and energy) and announces that Andy said he had Jesus in his heart, he is doing what Mummy does—pry into people's lives and ask them if they know Jesus. When I see him tucking in his shirt in a certain way I recognize it's because he "wants to be like Daddy." As independent and strong willed as he is, he still gets his sense of identity and belonging from the ones he spends most of his time with, his parents.

Both Ken and I are very aware of our special role in Jordan's life. We are the instruments (both male and female) God is using to form his value system. If we are nonexistent in any area of his life, then something else will fill the void. He will get his values one way or another, and his identity will be developed or underdeveloped by the ones he chooses to exercise. The habits he picks up from us will greatly determine his future character. Jordan has picked up our tastes (even rice and peanut sauce), our energy, our way of doing things, and our faith. By watching us he is getting a lesson on how men and women relate in a God-centered home; how a family led by the Lord lives. By accompanying me to the inner city and into the prison, he is learning how to care for people, particularly those who are geographically challenged and endure hardships.

This is the greatest tragedy in American history—an entire generation of young people who do not have decent parent models. Many of our young people no longer have respect for those who were put in the position of being their primary role model, and for good reason. The fathers and mothers of this land have abdicated their role as the first and most important heroes in each of their children's lives. Not the school teacher, not the pastor, and certainly not the boys in the hood. The parents. My siblings and I are who we are because of our parents. They were tough on us, but they loved and respected us and we loved and respected them. We listened to them because they took the time to listen to us and get into our lives. They valued us. We were all very special in their eyes, which made us special to one another. We were, and still are, one another's best friends.

Today, six of my seven siblings live within twenty minutes of each other, three live in the same apartment complex. I live the most central of us and am no more than ten minutes from any one of them. My brother Philip lives in London with his family, but our hopes are that they will join us soon. This is fascinating to me, because we were all born in Uganda. We all went abroad to study, some in London, others in America. We all had the choice to live in the many different countries and states we experienced, but we chose to live in the same city. Why? The family that prays together, stays together.

As far back as I can remember, our parents brought us together for prayer every day. Every evening, between 9:00 P.M. and 10:00 P.M. was the Wilson family prayer time. When my father was out of town my mother gathered us together in our living room. Everyone in the household had to be present, even the help if they weren't too busy. It was a sacred time in which misbehaviour was strictly forbidden. We would sing from hymn books, my brother Albert would play the piano. We would request our favourites, or my mother would teach us new ones. Then the Word of God was read and my father would expound on it and ask us questions. Then there would be a time of prayer, and we would close off the time singing the grace.

In case you are thinking that this was an easy task, let me

quickly tell you that it seemed like a nuisance to us sometimes, especially when our favourite T.V. program was on. My father's authority on the issue of evening prayer was absolute, but we had a friend in him, and we negotiated successfully most nights. Compromises within reason were often practiced. When necessary, my father never hesitated to use his magic. He would join us and watch and enjoy the program with us, then he would segue smoothly into devotions, taking us with him, willing captives.

My father and mother also had their own prayer time together every morning, and throughout the day you would see them reading their Bibles and having their own personal time with the Lord, then at night to close off the day. We saw our parents in action, serving others with joy. Theirs was a practical faith. They weren't perfect people, and we never enjoyed moving out of our rooms for guests, but their love made them perfect in our eyes.

My father placed the family he loved so dearly in the safest place he knew—in Jesus' hands, and Jesus has kept them together these many years after his death through the continuing influence of my mother. When I lost my father, God very graciously spared my mother. I thank Him daily that I still have my mother. As I have reflected on my father's death over the years I have come to the conclusion that even though I loved my father dearly, more dearly than any woman has ever loved her father, had God chosen to take my mother instead, it would have been more difficult to bear. She was the one who gave me life and that was a powerful connection I still needed. There was an invisible umbilical cord that I still needed to bring me wisdom and nurture as I myself became a wife and mother.

I have always respected my mother; she was and continues to be a woman of great accomplishments. The first-born of five sisters, she was an excellent student and graduated from Makerere University with a degree in Art. Her only problem was that she was too talented. As I struggle with how to juggle a career and possibly a second child, I am most impressed with the fact that my mother carried (for sixty-three months!), gave birth to (seven labours!), and successfully raised five boys and two girls while working on her art, teaching senior school, designing and making dresses, running her own bridal business, building a house, singing in a national choir, and, and..., all the while heavily involved with the revival movement beside my father!

I was her eldest of two daughters. We had the makings of a rocky relationship from the very beginning. We were two very strong women sharing the love of one very special man. Not only that, with five boys, she needed someone to sport her frilly creations; instead she was met with an adamant little tomboy who wanted to hide her lanky legs and little knob-knees in the plentiful supply of hand-me-down jeans and trousers. My sister, who adored little frilly dresses, didn't come to my rescue for another ten years.

My mother and I continued to endure the ups and downs of our unique relationship during the turbulent teenage years, and through my confused 'lost' years at college, and through it all we came out winners. My father's death brought us together in a special way, because we had both loved him terribly and we shared a blinding commitment to see his vision continue. Through what I can only imagine was hell for my mother, she resolved to go on and fulfill the promise she had made to my father minutes before his death—to take care of their children. She retreated to the Center to get the vision that would give her the strength to carry on. She became a great supporter and teacher to me. On my wedding day I proudly wore the beautiful masterpiece she had always wanted to create for me. We continue to be united in our faith and vision.

So what happens if you don't have those kinds of parents... is it a lost cause? Absolutely not. As long as there is still a hero in the land there is still hope. But it is our job to seek them out. God has placed heroes within reach of each of His children, but He wants us to develop some initiative and assertiveness to seek them out. We need good people to care about us, because when we are not valued by people of value, then we lose our self-esteem and turn to destructive behaviour. To seek out such people takes great spiritual discernment and prayer, but as we meet them, deep will speak to deep. Our spirits will unite in that unbreakable bond that survives time and distance.

My father's death left a big gap in my life, and as I looked around for a substitute Dad, I found out the Lord had already placed two very special heroes in my life who would continue to provide the fatherly wisdom and affirmation that I still needed. They were my father's two closest friends, one white the other black. One from South Africa, the other from Uganda. Michael Cassidy and Bishop Misaeri Kauma; two very special heroes.

These two men, both with families of their own, opened their hearts to my family in a remarkable way. They went to extraordinary lengths to help ease our grief and pain, even as they too grieved the loss of their dearest friend. They are solid men, men of tremendous faith, men of great vision, yet men of utmost graciousness and love. One led me to Christ, the other flew half way around the world to perform my wedding at great personal expense.

I feel like a daughter to these two men in every way and my love and respect for them is right up there with my father's. I take their advice and counsel very seriously, because they are men of amazing intellect and conscience and are highly esteemed in their circles. Like my father, they are eagles and God leads them into difficult places—on the front lines of the struggle for peace and reconciliation in their respective countries, and each day they continue to thrill and inspire me with their exploits. They are impressed only with radical Christianity, they demand it of themselves and they demand it of me. It is no wonder they were John Wilson's choice for friends. These are friends of substance. The world is a better place because they are in it.

I am a product of the East African revival movement, and

growing up I witnessed the joy of Jesus shine on the faces of men and women who were caught up in the worst persecution of this generation—that perpetrated upon the people of Uganda by a madman named Idi Amin. The Christians of Uganda found themselves with no freedoms on earth, but the love and joy they had discovered in Jesus made them 'free indeed.' No matter what the circumstances, they were heaven-bound. They faced their executioners with heads held high, singing praises to their God. Heroes.

Why has there suddenly fallen upon the earth a scarcity of such heroes of the Christian faith? Over the past few decades a dramatic leadership vacuum seems to have developed throughout every arena of Christendom. There is an absence of effective, compassionate, visionary leadership. Christian organizations are desperately calling out for men and women with leadership qualities and commitment to help them advance the cause of Christ. Where are all the men and women who were supposed to pick up the mantles of heroes such as Martin Luther, John Wesley, William Booth, William Carey, John Calvin, John Wycliff, D.L. Moody, and the list goes on? Who is being prepared by the Lord to take over from our own greats such as Billy Graham and Mother Theresa?

The Christian eagle population in the sky is getting very thin. We are being overrun by wicked little demons who are right at home in the skies over our heads. Outnumbered in a sea of demons, heroes have a reputation of dying prematurely and are usually difficult to insure in human terms, but to them the quantity of time is not as important as the quality. And quite frankly, they know no other way to live except on the cutting edge. The love of Christ drives them. They courageously challenge the devil in the fight to reclaim all the territory stolen from Christ. Setting the captives free.

Where are the spiritual risk takers? The men and women who aren't afraid to die? Where have all the heroes gone? As I have sought for the answer to this question, it has become clear to me that the greatest cry of the Holy Spirit today is for spiritual Indiana Joneses. Jesus is looking for more men and women who will take on the leadership of His Church today in the same way as the first disciples, "...they were praising God, and having favour with all people. And the Lord was adding to their number day by day those who were being saved." Acts 2:47.

Richard Foster, in his book *Celebration Of Discipline* says, "In our day heaven and earth are on tiptoe waiting for the emerging of a Spirit-led, Spirit-intoxicated, Spirit-empowered people." Christianity is no longer the mysterious and awe-inspiring faith demonstrated by believers such as Francis of Assisi; it seems to have become a morally bankrupt, moneymaking machine run by a bunch of false prophets and spiritual losers. The current crop of leaders is parading across the stage of our generation under the deep scrutiny of the Holy Spirit. What is He looking for? Gifts and talents? No! Character, discipline, maturity, responsibility, strength, courage, and greatest of all, love.

As Jesus walks through this land He again sees people who are distressed and downcast like sheep without a shepherd. The harvest is indeed plentiful, and He asks us again to pray for more workers, because we have plenty of managers and supervisors, but the labourers are few. We have plenty of volunteers to work within the comfort and confines of the church, but not enough servants out in the field, leading the charge in bringing in the harvest.

Why? Because there aren't enough leaders who pray. They are adept at talking to God for about five to ten minutes a day, but very poor in listening. No one is interested in what God has to say anymore. Instead, selfishness prevails and foolishness is the course of the day. It is easier to cut the missionary and evangelistic budgets of the church rather than listen to God and cut back on their salaries. They chase out the prophets, and get rid of the evangelists, and in so doing stifle the Holy Spirit out of their churches and they die.

God is again preparing leaders who are mature enough to hear

His voice for themselves and responsible enough to obey what He says. Radical servants. Nonconformists. Life-Bringers. The people that will change the world of their time. Their ears are fine tuned to hear their Master say, "I WILL NEVER DESERT YOU, NOR WILL I EVER FORSAKE YOU." Hebrews 13:5. To which they confidently respond with their creed, "THE LORD IS MY HELPER, I WILL NOT BE AFRAID. WHAT SHALL MAN DO TO ME?" Hebrews 13:6.

Richard Foster continues to say in his chapter on The Discipline of Guidance: "Individuals can be found here and there whose hearts burn with divine fire. But they are like flaming torches scattered in the night. As yet there has been no gathering of a people of the Spirit." Every time I feel like giving up on revival ever happening in America, I am reminded of the few flaming torches that are boldly speaking out for a Christ-centered life. Wonderful men and women of God, many of whom I have never met or had personal contact with, but under whose teaching I submit myself often, if not daily. I make it a point to be taught by people my spirit affirms as men and women of faith, integrity, wisdom and proven character. I read their books, listen to their voices on the radio, or from their tapes, and occasionally I catch them on television, though I haven't quite acquired a taste for T.V. evangelism.

I receive great blessings from these great teachers, particularly Dr. Dobson of Focus on the Family, for whom I work my schedule around daily not only because he cares about the same things I care about, but also because he gives other people of vision a forum to share their dreams. All the people who capture his attention have one goal in common, for "Our Father's Kingdom to come on earth and His will to be done on earth as it is in heaven." Matthew 6:10.

Of course, the star that shines the brightest on the American landscape is that of Dr. Billy Graham, and I never miss a chance to listen (or watch) him, because he never fails to evoke such pride and awe in me. A Moses for our generation; even in his seventies he is still pure inspiration. He is the reason why I cannot write a chapter on heroes and not make a plea to our gray-haired soldiers who, after fighting a good fight, have slipped quietly back into the chicken pen. Nothing disappoints me more than to see the elders of this country sitting in retirement homes believing they are good only for prayer. Mind you, no one lives to pray more than I, because to me prayer is as vital and necessary as breathing. But why should there come a time when the shoes are put away and all we can do is pray?

I believe this is a myth that the devil has perpetrated to eliminate the older saints from the role of teaching the young people and being sign posts along their way. Instead, medicated and with poor circulation due to lack of exercise and fresh air, they are tucked away from a society that considers them an eyesore. These are the men and women who should be sitting at the gates of this great nation being the imparters of wisdom that they are supposed to be, but they, believing they are no longer useful, have relinquished their powers to the younger generation who covertly enact laws to kill them off before their time. These half-baked chickens are riding this magnificent country to hell in a hand basket, while the Christian elderly sit in their chairs with blank stares waiting for God to take them home. Even the prayers they are assigned to pray lose their flavour and become a chore, and their hearts become bitter and stubborn.

This is a wake up call to our veteran heroes. This is a war that must be fought to the death. There is no such thing as spiritual retirement. You must recapture your joy in the Lord, because the battle being waged against our youth cannot wait for you to sit back and say, "I don't have a song anymore," or "I'm tired; it's my turn to live my life." Lift up your eyes and look on the fields, that they are white with harvest. More accurately, the harvest has been left so long it's rotting! It is evil. I have never met a more undisciplined, insolent, destructive force of mishandled man power as the lost generation. With each Christian light that is snuffed out, it is the young people who suffer from the resulting darkness. Now they have completely lost their way. We have a nation of young people who are so full of despair that their hearts have turned to stone. They are unfeeling, walking civil wars.

Somebody has to get mad and do something about it. We are Christians. We have the gospel! And the gospel is the only answer because it never changes! Jesus saved in the past, He saves today, and He will continue to save in the future. The young people in this country and all over the world need that message as they have never needed it before. If you don't take it to them, then who will? What difference is it how old the vessel is, Jesus can still use it. The love that pours out is the same, and they need your love, your attention, your wisdom, your encouragement and your guidance.

Heroes, if you are listening...God is calling again. If you feel you have been inactive too long, take heart, your wings are polished and ready. As long as a man or woman of God still has breath in their lungs, they still have verses in their song to sing. God's timing is perfect. When your song is over, He will take you home and give you a standing ovation. The choruses of heaven will rise up in joy and praise you for a song well sung, even to the last note. Don't run out of steam before you hit that last note, and hit it with as much gusto as the first note you ever uttered. Get back in the fight. It's never too late. Get out of that house and find some desperate young people in your church or nearby school, or half-way house, or prison, or hospital and reclaim them before they hit the cemetery, for once they're there it's too late; you've lost the chance to sing that line in your song at great cost to that poor person who was waiting desperately to hear it.

Show them your Jesus. Teach them how to love again. Teach them how to find value in themselves again. Find for yourself fresh waters and turn your last years into the most productive years of your life. If your nest is empty, open it up for new eaglets anxiously wanting to learn to fly the right way. Help prepare a generation for tomorrow's leadership.

It's a sad day in America, which translates as a sad day for the world, because the rest of the world serves as the dumping ground for all the filth that's generated from the degenerate minds that are the product of a Godless society. If America does not change it's moral campus it is because the elders preferred their comfort over going back to where they lost the ball and working to pass it on. We can't ask the youth, we mustn't ask the youth. They don't have the weapons. They are ill-equipped. Too dysfunctional. The concept of grabbing the vision for themselves and carrying it on is moot if they don't even have the faintest idea what it is they are supposed to be striving after. I, for one, am going to fight to see that revival happens somewhere in America because I love the children—they deserve a better chance, a better environment to grow and develop in.

If, however, all you manage to produce as the future generation is simply fodder for hell, then I am returning to Africa to raise up an army to take a stand against your morals, your movies, your music, your pornography, your diseases, your drugs, your killing of the unborn, your arrogance, your social disorder, your racism, your wimpy Christianity, against anything you wish to sell us, or dump on us that comes from hell. If you don't value your children enough to fight for them, to teach and raise them up in the way they should go, then we shall fight to save ours from yours.

You are reaping the seeds of your lack of responsibility to the generation that came after you. You failed to discipline them and to teach them to respect their elders, so you lost them. Now they are perpetuating the same evil upon their children that you unleashed upon them, and they in turn are unleashing it back on you. Abuse of the elderly in this country has risen to mammoth proportions; it's too painful to even comprehend the extent of it. It's time to fight back. You must fight for both of them, your children and their children. It is never too late with God. You must take out your hero attitude, wrap it around yourself and be a hero to all those coming up behind you.

Africa is the continent of the future for the gospel of Jesus Christ. We are banishing hell and shall let it have no part in our future. If we can't march into the twenty-first century together with you and those whom God has given you to lead, then we shall have to go without you. But we shall go with clear consciences because we were willing to give up our lives to bring you the gospel of peace. We left our homelands to come and share with you the joy that you have lost, the power that comes from simple faith, the thrill of falling in love again with your first love. You can no longer claim ignorance. You can no longer polish off old medals of service; you must go out and win new ones.

If, amidst all the clamour and haste of America, you refuse to listen once more to the still, small voice calling you to be the heroes you were meant to be, then we shall mourn for you for a season, and then move on. My prayer is that we all go on together, those who led us and those whom we are leading, holding high the cross of Jesus. Onward Christian soldiers...marching to war.

Chapter 14

A Test of the Emergency Broadcasting System

There is one thing to which neither man or woman dare turn a blind eye: the anointing of the Holy Spirit which alone fits them to speak for God.

Corrie ten Boom

After the LIFE-BRINGERS period I was so totally disenchanted with the college group I felt it was finally time to leave. I could not wring blood out of a turnip. It was not an easy decision because I had invested so much time in the college group and I desperately wanted to see the revival start there. I was saddened that only a few of those young people had caught the fire, but they had allowed me to grow and be tested by the Lord in preparation for the next stage of my training.

A rather curious pattern was now beginning to emerge in the way the Lord worked. I had not yet been able to outguess Him. To stretch me He always presented a vision just out of reach so I could exercise my fullest potential, then He would work it out in a way that always left me flabbergasted, in absolute awe of His power and faithfulness. The results I expected out of my visions were never the results I received. His results came complete with showers of blessings. Love would flood my heart, my soul would sing with renewed hope and courage, and my feet would take on a new spring. Grace would abound all around me.

Before I left the group I waited for a clear signal from the

Lord. One Sunday morning at around 4:30 a.m. I was awakened by the Lord. Not realizing it, I tried to go back to sleep, but I couldn't. I was wide awake, so I tuned my mind to the prayer wave. Did you call, my Lord?

"I want you to go and tell them to repent and turn to me, otherwise I will remove the blessing."

I was just dreaming that I was awake, was my first thought. I pinched myself. I was awake. I listened to the vital signs in the room. My husband was breathing calmly beside me, and so was my son in his cot at the foot of our bed. Lord, I am pleading with you, how can I go in there and say that? And what blessing are you talking about? I can't. I don't ever want to stand up again in front of that group, so unless you have another method of delivery, I'm going back to sleep. Thankfully, sleep came for another hour before I was awakened again.

"Tell the leaders that if their message today is not on repentance, they must scrap it and call those young people to their knees before me. I am giving them one last chance before I remove My hand from them."

Not wanting to be disobedient I showed up early at the group meeting the next day and holding Ken's hand firmly I tremblingly shared the message with the college pastor and his assistant. They both smiled at me sweetly and thanked me for the message, then proceeded on with business as usual. I wept silently through the service for the group for I realized what the blessing was. The mantle I had inherited from my father. The Lord was removing me from the group and with me went the mantle. On the tragic day he died, my father was shot four times; two of the bullets hit major arteries in the upper thigh and the spleen, he died from loss of blood. He shed it all. The seed he had died that day to plant had been rejected in this group; the Lord would find another field with good soil. Perhaps a different group within the church, or possibly even a new church.

Ken, meanwhile, was happily serving in the pre-kindergarten class, so I tried that for a short while. Although I enjoyed the children and they offered me a chance to work on my performance skills, they did not offer me the intellectual and spiritual challenge I yearned for. Ken and I visited different Sunday school groups. We tried the one for young marrieds—too young. A thirty something group—a little too much angst, I did not feel equipped for their unique type of pain. The singles group didn't even want me to speak there; "Where she is going is not where we are going." I bid them bon voyage.

Then I found myself writing messages in my journal for the leadership of our church. I had great confidence in our pastors. Most of them were men who had known my father and had believed in his message. Now I didn't want to pay attention to what I felt the Lord was asking me to do. He wanted to move me on to the 'seat of power' to encourage the leadership to stay on track. Apparently the passion had developed a leak and too many compromises were being made. The focus was turning financial to the detriment of the message.

I had no great desire to play ball with the 'big boys,' that was the kind of stress I could do without, I had enough with my preschooler. Besides, this was a congregation that had a lot of problems and I did not want to enter into their politics. Gone were the golden days of the corner church that sent missionaries the world over and listened to all messages from God no matter through whom He chose to speak. We were still sending missionaries, but now we were the grand buildings that took up half a city block. We were millions of dollars in debt and very low on the joy that had once characterized the soul of our church.

We had become comfortable. No fireworks, no rocking of the boat. We had become sanitized, sterilized, complacent and impotent. Now God was threatening to come down and start a revival. He wanted them to clean house, beginning with the leadership and the priesthood. I was soon to find out that this was not on their agenda, and prophets and evangelists were not necessarily seen as gifts from God. Billy Graham, at a Conference for Itinerant Evangelists, said that a church without an evangelist is a dead or dying church.

Certainly we had died in our spirits. We had forgotten to love. Several members were upset with the ethnic mix that was taking place in the church. 'Those people' were clapping a little too loudly and were disturbing their composure. They wrote the pastor nasty, mean-spirited letters decrying the new songs being introduced that had a little too much soul. They made threats to withdraw their rather sizable support if this was not rectified.

Apart from two or three well-known male speakers of colour a year, there was a dearth of ethnic representation from the pulpit...and in the priesthood, too, for that matter. Yet this big, magnificent church was located in a heavily ethnic area. It's potential to lead the way in racial healing was incredible. It had the potential to start the revival I was so desperate to see in America. But it was not a neighbourhood church, and its convenient access to the freeway allowed the people to enter and leave without any contact with the neighbourhood. Now the inevitable was happening, the neighbourhood was spilling into the church and many members resented it.

As a woman I faced another challenge. The many years I worked with the college group had shielded me to a certain extent from the sexism within the church, because there I had been allowed to exercise my gifts. I was given many wonderful opportunities to speak as openly as I felt the Lord leading. In the greater church I now encountered talk that some women in the congregation were upset that women were being allowed to pray from the pulpit. I could not even hope for a public ministry from that pulpit; I was better off with the college group.

Yet who was I to say no to the Lord? If He wanted me to come alongside the leadership, as a sort of prophet to the church, then that is what I would do. Encouraging the pastor was first on the list of duties. In my first contacts with him I told him that the Lord had revealed to me that there was sin in the priesthood and that the Lord wanted him, as the pastor, to crack down on it. Once the priesthood was sanctified and holy, then he was to call the people to repentance before the Almighty God. I felt he took the message seriously.

In one particular sermon he gave upon his return from a vacation, he had both barrels smoking. He was back and ready to take care of business for the Lord. He called the racists on their tactics and nasty letters, he called the sinners in the sin, and called the complacent back to love. I was never more proud of him as I was at that moment, and I immediately told him so. I walked away from the church smiling. It wasn't so bad playing with 'the big boys' if they, too, were playing according to God's will. I still have a copy of that tape.

Then I started receiving messages for the church and, as usual, I tried to reason with the Lord. After all, hadn't He appointed a shepherd over His people for this very purpose? Reluctantly, I approached the leadership on the possibility of my having five minutes to speak to the congregation. We could call it 'a congregational moment,' or 'a lay witness,' or 'a testimony,' whatever would not offend the congregation. I wanted to be sensitive to their position. As it turned out, it was never the 'right time' nor the 'right audience.'

My hands were tied. There was nothing to do except grieve that I could give this wake-up call to other congregations, but not mine. I was jealous for my church; I believed it had been ordained by God for a time such as this and I longed to see the Holy Spirit literally fall upon us and set our feet on fire. I didn't see what difference it made whether the Lord used a man or a woman to bring this about. In Christ there were no distinctions, no Greek nor Jew, male nor female, no bond nor free.

Refusing the word of God on any terms was a foolish thing to do, especially for a church desperately in need of renewal. Even though the church calender was chock full of activities and finely organized programs, no renewal was evident. I knew that all the teaching in the world was simply vanity if there wasn't fundamental renewal in each of our hearts. We needed to break, to be poured out, to be cleansed and put back together. We needed to be filled with the Holy Spirit. We needed to go before the Lord in humility and repent of our wimpy Christianity.

If I thought waking up the college group had been painful, it was nothing compared to waking up the greater church. To the unsuspecting lay person, my words were seen as unloving and critical of the establishment which, as far as they were concerned, was saying and doing the right things. I was the dangerous one, the heretic, the self-righteous one. Jesus kept reminding me that this was typical fare for prophets. I could expect to lose even more of the few supporters I had left within the church, possibly even some very close friends. I now had to trust only in the Lord. He had to be my everything.

I got inspiration from Lady Thatcher of whom it was once said, "...better an Iron Lady than those cardboard men." It was time for God's Iron Ladies to stand up and lead the way back to the water. Someone had to wake the people up to the fact that there was only one Master Plan - "If My people..." That's when 'the idea' hit me!

My first response was, "No. Absolutely not. Idea dismissed." I tried to block the image out of my mind, hoping desperately that it was a 'me' thought. 'Me' thoughts eventually went away if ignored. 'God' thoughts never did in spite of everything I did to avoid them, and they all came to me the same way—as a simple thought...a simply crazy thought that I immediately tried to toss out. If it persisted in my mind, then started to occupy my prayer life and my study time, and my every other time, then it was time to pay attention. But this idea was preposterous. The Lord would never ask me to do such a thing. And there was no way I would do it. It was way off the boldness meter.

A couple of days after this particular 'simple thought' entered my consciousness, a little bell started ringing in my head and I began to panic. The idea was rapidly turning into a vision. I began to see it. I could see myself in it. I could see the place, the people, the time of day. I started mouthing the words I was to speak. The harder I pushed it into my subconscious, the harder it fought to take center stage. I turned to my husband, Ken, and jokingly asked him what he thought about my getting up Sunday morning and speaking to the congregation, uninvited? He told me I was either crazy or called by God.

I opted for crazy. At least that didn't demand obedience. The idea could remain safely in my mind, and I would stay safely in my comfort zone. Then my Bible readings and journal entries began to focus on the message, convincing me that God really was calling me to do this; after all, hadn't I exhausted all other conventional means of getting it to the people?

In all my eight years as a member of that church the thought of just taking the time had never crossed my mind. I had thought of leaving many times, but never this. Our church was so organized it was airtight. The three services, averaging 1,000 to 1,500 people each, were pieced together in minute detail. The organist knew exactly when to tiptoe in and out. The music was soft, gentle, 'upright,' carefully chosen to be engaging, but not to disturb. Everything was very timely and orderly. My intrusion would be seen as nothing short of a terrorist attack. I could see the headlines: "Fifteen hundred people taken hostage by a woman from Africa proclaiming the message of the Cross at a time when it has almost ceased to be referred to in the pulpits of America."

It would be a God-take-over. As outrageous as it seemed, I had to admit that this was possibly what it was going to take to revive a church whose vital signs were approaching Code Blue— they needed shock therapy. Certainly, the alarm clock had been ringing so long they had become immune to it.

To ease my anxiety, I dared to dream that once they encountered Jesus, even those staunch 'upright' pillars would loosen up and start to sing and dance before their God. Finally Jesus would be glorified in our church, and we would be known for our love. God would revive His church into action. Together we would proclaim the message of love and reconciliation to our needy city. We would feed the hungry, visit the sick, free the captives, and mend the brokenhearted. What an incredible vision. We would really march for Jesus then, every day, in my favourite places; the prisons and inner cities of this great nation. There where the deepest of pain lay, there the greatest need for Jesus was to be found. And there was Jesus, and His servants with Him.

They say that if it seems too good to be true then it probably is. This seemed like an impossible dream, but when it came to the God I served, I knew nothing was impossible. Big dreams, impossible dreams, parting-of-the-Red-Sea dreams, those were the kind the Lord loved. But in this case, I knew I would never make it out of my seat without fainting. Not that I lacked courage; I walked into the inner city every Saturday afternoon wearing fatigues, my partners and I holding a wooden cross and different signs for Jesus. Once or twice a week I went into the Los Angeles Men's Central Jail and visited men in maximum security, locked in cages like animals. Hardened criminals with records a mile long. I was open to any new challenges the Lord would send my way, but this...this would take courage the likes of which I had never entertained.

Yet the Lord seemed to be telling me that He was no respecter of persons. No one decided for Him when the time was right or when it was the right audience. He didn't need an invitation to get His point across; He had demonstrated that with the hand writing across the wall that brought Belshazzar's party in Daniel 5 to a serious halt. The sight had all but done the poor man in. At His appointed time, God was going to make a way for me to speak to His people. I just had to be in church Sunday morning at 9:00 A.M. and wait for His call.

I was now in full panic, my throttle resonating on every nerve in my body. Ken was behind me one hundred percent; he knew God had placed this on my heart, but he, too, had to admit that this was way off the scales, even for me. However, it was his confidence in me and that kept me going, because I had lost all mine.

On Wednesday, December 29, 1993, I wrote in my journal: "Circumcise yourselves to the LORD, circumcise your hearts... or My wrath will break out and burn like fire. Sound the trumpet throughout the land!" Jeremiah 4:4 & 5. After those verses, I wrote in bold letters across the page - "IT IS TIME TO TAKE BACK AMERICA FOR JESUS! RAISE THE SIGNAL TO GO TO ZION!" I had to do it, God had called me. He wanted His church back. There was just one little problem—He gave me no guarantee that this time they would heed the message. They could totally reject it and drag me out, or they could embrace it and turn their hearts back to God. I just had to be obedient and leave the consequences to Him.

The time had come to ask for 'uncommon faith.' Jesus was asking me to strip myself completely of self and place my faith totally in Him. He was in total control of the situation, and He was still a God of order. He would orchestrate that morning's service, He would give me the energy to stand up and walk to the microphone. He would use my mind and my mouth to say exactly what He wanted to say. Then He would walk me back to my seat, and it would be over.

I lost my appetite. I became listless. I sighed big agonized sighs. I read the Bible hoping to find a ram in the thicket, but all the passages I read seemed to start with "Tell this to the nations," "Proclaim it to Jerusalem." I hid in Ken's arms and found great comfort in his words as he put me before the Throne of mercy. He was amazed at the anguish I was going through. I spent every single second I could before the Lord, taking down the message, several pages a day. I was reminded of Maya Angelou who said she had crystallized those five minutes of magnificent poetry she gave at President Clinton's Inauguration out of pages and pages of material she had first put down. I knew the Lord would say whatever He needed to say, preferably in five minutes or less.

I shared the burden with those closest to me, my prayer warriors, and the battle began in earnest. I felt that a decision that had the potential of landing me in the hospital with a nervous breakdown warranted the counsel of many, but I was not prepared for what I found. They were split down the middle, the same number for as against. Those for it immediately aligned themselves beside me, validating my call and vowing their support. Those against immediately began to give me reasons why it would be a disastrous move and gave me several elementary suggestions on what they felt the Lord was telling me to do.

I began to see clearly where eagles differed from foot soldiers. An eagle's view was aerial, he/she saw more of the picture. He was keenly aware of the fact that the only reason he was even in the air was because of the Wind beneath his wings. An eagle was never delusional as to whose war this was. The foot soldiers saw the church and its traditions, they saw the people and were worried about how the message would be received. Their view tended to be on the situation and not on what God could do in the hearts of His people. Their concern for safety and man-perceived order did not reflect an eagle's understanding of the inherent risk of God-inspired progress and the resulting joy of victory.

Out of desperation, I made a deal with the Lord. I would ask one last time for those five minutes. If my request was dismissed again, then I would do whatever the Lord wanted. I called and after a joyless, perfunctory exchange of words, I was dismissed with an emotionless, "We'll pray about it," that lacked the conviction or integrity I was hoping for. My anger at being dismissed so negatively was abated by the fact that we were having a guest speaker that particular Sunday. I had some breathing space, at least for that week.

I went to church as usual, sat in my usual place and was totally blessed by the guest speaker. Although there seemed to be no immediate tangible transformation in the congregation I felt the message had gone out, the call had been given. It had certainly touched me. I prayed that many would take it home on an individual level and we would soon see it rippling through the church. I could hope, couldn't I? I was reminded that the rules were already set by God, and I still had to play my part. I was not to fear because He had already made provision for the vision.

I spent the next week see-sawing back and forth trying to sort out the signals. By Friday afternoon I had talked myself out of it. I didn't want to die just yet. I asked Ken to take us away for a weekend...as far away as possible. As soon as I made that decision it seemed like God removed His presence from me. He sent me to the 'think tank' (1990s version of the belly of the fish) to mull it over. The decision was so heavy on my heart I could hardly stand it. I felt a need to cry. I reached out to God, but couldn't feel Him. Life lost its light. I may not have died physically like Jesus or Jonah, but for all intents and purposes I may as well have been dead.

Late that night, I broke down and started to sob; deep, uncontrollable sobs. The depth of my pain took me by surprise; I had not cried so deeply since several months before when the Lord had led me away from the college group and closed the door. What was this grief for now? The church? Was God closing His door on the whole church? Was He finally going to move me out and send me home, or to a new church?

I was old and tired, but I would willingly start all over again from scratch at another church, because I hated going to mine. I hated the sterilized services and the forever messages on finances. Once again I tried to reason with the Lord. How could this call be from Jesus? I had been taught to believe that a call from God came with peace of mind. Where was the lightness in this burden? Had my eyes not been producing tears faster than I could dry them, I might have seen Jesus standing quietly beside me. As my moaning subsided, I heard His voice.

"Don't run away. Stay and do this for me."

I continued crying silently, my mouth twisted, my heart still very heavy. I didn't see how I could do it. I couldn't stand up in the middle of the service and give the message. I knew we still had a long way to go before my fellow church members reached the point of understanding that would allow them to receive a message brought to them in such an unorthodox way.

As I laboured in the spirit, I distinctly remember catching a glimpse of Jesus, and I say 'glimpse' because the spiritual impression of His presence was so strong on my mind and my soul that it was almost visible, then it disappeared. My father had forever been 'catching a sight of Jesus.' Is this what he had meant? It didn't change my decision to leave town, but it greatly restored my faith. He was still there, even as I traveled through the valley of the shadow of death. He would never leave me, not for a second.

But why couldn't I shake this depression? I just leaned over the kitchen sink and bawled. Where was Father God? Where was the Comforter? "Dear Lord, it's me, Victoria. Why have you turned your back on me?" Jesus now watched me quietly from the sofa, then looked away. "Look at me, Lord, look at me!" I croaked, "I'm in a very dark place and I can't even tell you why. All I know is that my heart is sick. I don't know where you are. I can't live like this. Death would be quite welcome just about now. Please show me your face again." In the stillness of the darkness came the gentle voice.

"Stay and fight."

Okay, okay, okay! Anything but this. If you want me to do this, then I will. I will get up and do exactly as You lead.

Immediately I felt the burden of fear lift! Again the working of the Holy Spirit caught me off guard. Tremendous peace filled my heart. If I just followed His orders all would be well, I had nothing to fear for no weapon formed against me would prosper. I imagined Jesus freezing all the ushers and security guards in place and allowing me to peacefully give the message. Strength filled my heart. I put on some music and danced around the room swinging my sword at all the demons that had been threatening to destroy me through their devious oppression. This one belonged to Jesus.

I sat in my same place on Sunday, but Jesus didn't call me. Instead, that following week I received an invitation to speak at the church that ran my son's preschool. That was the first of thirteen messages I gave at that church as their interim speaker. It was a beginning of a beautiful relationship that was to teach me what a fellowship of believers was really about.

I had asked for uncommon faith. I felt like I was on solid ground. I knew without a shadow of a doubt that even though I would get knocked down in some of the battles, the war belonged to Jesus. I had been tested in a way I would never forget, but for the faith that it produced I thank God I had been found faithful.

Chapter 15

What is it Going to Take?

The more I live - the more I learn
The more I learn - the more I realize
The less I know
Each step I take --
    (Papa, I've a voice now!)
Each page I turn --
    (Papa, I've a choice now!)
Each mile I travel only means
The more I have to go.

What's wrong with wanting more?
If you can fly - then soar!
With all there is - why settle for
Just a piece of sky?

Papa, I can hear you...
Papa, I can see you...
Papa, I can feel you...
Papa, watch me fly!

    Barbra Streisand, YENTL

Perhaps no other movie has had a greater effect on me than Barbra Streisand's *Yentl*. At its release I was twenty-five, and working in a bank. A girlfriend/coworker and I sat mesmerized through *Yentl* nine times. We saw it in 75mm Dolby sound at the Dome on Sunset Boulevard. We saw it in a small theater on Fairfax Avenue. We followed it all over Los Angeles. We couldn't get enough of it. We bought the album, and even snuck a tape recorder into a theater to record it. We listened to the tapes and quoted the movie at work, we literally built a life around Yentl for several months.

During that period I conceived the idea to produce a calendar to celebrate the beauty and diversity of the African woman. Everybody in the world told me it was impossible. Yentl kept telling me, "nothing is impossible." For that lesson, I will always be indebted to Barbra Streisand, for with that phrase ringing in my ears, I worked on the calendar for two years and in 1985, *AFRICA THE WOMAN* rolled off the presses.

My father saw this as a major accomplishment and was very proud of the way I had incorporated my education and talents with my cultural awareness. He died with proud thoughts of me. He had seen a little of what I could do. He had seen me fly, and that has meant a lot to me over the years. I have just built on that foundation, hoping and praying that I will never do anything to lessen his trust in me. Now, nine years later, as I look towards my second venture into publishing, it is no longer Yentl who assures me that nothing is impossible, it is God who tells me all things are possible through Him.

Jesus and I are at the computer again. He sits in His usual place beside my desk reading through some of the chapters of the book. He is in no hurry. He isn't going anywhere and He knows I'm not either. He just wants me to be very clear about our mission so that we have no encumbrances along the way, so He asks me...again;

"What do you really want to say?"

As I approach the last rewrite of the last chapter of the book I must weigh through what I have already written. Have I said everything I wanted to say? Is there more I still want to say? What do I want to say anyway? What do **we** want to see accomplished through this book?

Jesus and I have spent many long hours over this manuscript in the last year and a half. Together we have tested every word, every thought, every memory, every emotion, every intention. We have worked at all hours of the day. There have been several 5:00 A.M. nights and 5:00 A.M. mornings. But it has been wonderful. I have never felt so sure of the Wind beneath my wings.I have never devoured Scripture like I have done in this period of my life. I have never been so intimate with Jesus. My love for Him has grown so real and so deep that I am literally consumed by it. I can't help it. I can't stop it. I must always talk about Him.

"So that's what you really want to say?"

Yes. I love You. That's what I want to tell the world. I thank You for Ken. I thank You for Jordan. I thank You for everything you have blessed me with so tremendously, but most of all for You. For Your love for me. For my love for You. You have been faithful. You have given me everything I have asked for and much, much more. Having You here just sitting with me makes me feel like the richest woman in the world.

"Even with only $15 in your bank account?"

Even with a zero balance. I can't draw love from my bank account, I can only draw that from You. You are and will always be the only one who can pay my price. All the 'bank' in Switzerland can't begin to touch what I have in You. All the 'fame' in Hollywood can't hold a candle to the fire You have set in me. Yes, that's what I want to say...how wonderful is the name of Jesus. That is a conviction I hold without compromise, because it is not up for sale. It is not up for debate.

We sit quietly as I praise Him in my spirit. I am so glad we don't need words, because there are no words to say what I feel with the same eloquence as the spirit. "... Listen, listen to me, and eat what is good, and your soul will delight in the richest of fare." Isaiah 55:2. His presence in my life is so sweet. I glance at the almost ready manuscript, now over two hundred pages strong. He didn't bring me this far to let me down. He will finish the book. He knows exactly what we must say as we prepare to finish it. I relax and take stock of my weapons; four translations of the Bible, my journal, a dictionary, an exhaustive concordance, J.I.

Packer's book *Knowing God*, the book *Heritage of Freedom*--an illustrated guide to radical movements in Christian history, and *Together In One Place*--the story of PACLA.

PACLA.

The Pan African Christian Leadership Assembly. This historic assembly brought over 800 Christian leaders from all over Africa together in Nairobi, Kenya, December 9-19, 1976. My father and several key people including Michael Cassidy and Gottfried Osei-Mensah (the writers of *Together In One Place*), and many, many others including Billy Graham, joined hands together and pulled off one of the major coups in the history of Christianity in Africa. With the major load of co-ordinating the assembly, my father and his colleague, Andre Massaki, criss-crossed Africa encouraging the brethren in different churches, denominations, and language groups to respond to the call of the Lord and come together. This was my father's first major victory after seminary, and its impact was felt by more than just the people that were at the assembly; it also impacted me and changed my life.

Many wonderful people made PACLA happen, but to me PACLA was my father. He knew that it was a difficult time for me, alone for the first time in a big country, so he sent me letters from different countries in Africa, listing the countries he had just been in and the ones where he was going. Each letter brought me into a closer awareness of that beautiful continent and the many wonderful people that lived on it, and I decided I wanted to spend my life serving Africa. I changed my major from music to communications to better meet the needs of this complex continent.

Jesus picks up my journal and starts to skim through it. I'm not alarmed. He does this quite frequently. I am not ashamed of anything I've written. Jesus reads one of the sentences out loud.

> ***"I am absolutely, completely, unashamedly, unequivocally saved to the bone..."***

I've made some revisions to that statement. Now I'm saved to the marrow, if that's possible. He smiles and shakes His head. I'm so glad He knows my heart, because even if I'm accused of madness (a la Joan of Arc) by those who don't understand what it's like to be captured by His love, at least Jesus knows I'm only hopelessly in love with Him. The most preferred of all altitudes to an eagle, and the most jealously guarded.

He closes the journal and sets it on His knees. It isn't often He gets this kind of absolute love and devotion from one of His sheep. He stops to enjoy the moment. He looks at me. There are tears in my eyes. There are tears in His eyes.

"But it's not enough, is it?"

What can I say? I love you with all my heart, but I miss Africa something awful. I haven't been back in over eight years. I haven't seen my father's grave since they finished it, all I've seen are pictures. I feel like there's a hole in my heart. I just want to visit, to sit quietly beside the grave, to surround it with flowers, to remind the people of the sacrifice. I want to see and to be a part of the new Uganda; to experience his dream becoming a reality as our nation now emerges out of the ashes to be the true success story of Africa. I just want to eat an African pineapple, to savour some sauteed grasshoppers, to see an African sunset and experience an African night. Is that too much to ask? Haven't I been faithful? Don't I deserve that? It can only be good for my soul.

Perfect love. I know He understands me and loves me anyway. That's what I love about Him. I don't have to make appointments with Him, or be perfectly made-up. I don't have to perform and quickly think up great sounding words to put together. I don't have to guess at what He wants to hear. He doesn't laugh at my sentence construction. I can draw on all He has to offer just by waiting on Him, by being in His presence, keeping my mind stayed on Him. These are the times when the Bible springs alive in my heart and mind. These are the times when I am fortified so no lofty thing can be raised up against the knowledge of God.

"I would have despaired..."

I finish it for Him, "...unless I had believed that I would see the goodness of the Lord in the land of the living. Wait for the Lord, be strong, and let your heart take courage; yes, wait for the Lord." Psalm 27:13 and 14. To want something so desperately only to be told to wait is what the cross is all about. To have a faith so strong to believe that He will give me the desires of my heart in accordance to His good and perfect will.

The happiest people on earth are those who know how blessed they are, because their eyes are not on their circumstances, their eyes are on the Lord. When your treasure is Jesus, you sing praises from the heart, thanking God for all the joy He's given you. It will happen. I know it will, and in His perfect timing. Impatience is the killer of joy, and besides, we still have a book to finish. I have no idea what the outcome of that will be. There are no guarantees, but there is trust that He is already there preparing the way, just as He is with me now.

As my attention turns back to PACLA, something which has bothered me throughout the writing of this book is now brought to the forefront. Because I have lived in America for over half of my life, the book has addressed mostly American issues, as a result I feel like I have not addressed my African brothers and sisters as directly as I have wanted to. This saddens me because this book was originally written to African women.

Yet I cannot pretend to really understand their struggles not having lived through the nightmares of war. Many are caught up in very complex situations in which I dare not try to offer advice. However, one universal need I know is that we all want to know what our life is all about; we need to know that we are worth more than what the world tells us, and that we are here for a reason and a purpose--life is not in vain. Most of us just want a good, decent life as defined by the culture in which we live, and a chance to raise healthy, happy children and be a productive, contributing member to society. I still believe in the goodness of man, and maintain that there are many more good people in this world than bad. Many good people are bad simply because of survival. They are not equipped nor given a chance to experience anything else.

Again my thoughts return to PACLA, to Africa. It is there that I am to receive the message with which to close this book. What is it going to take, Lord? You alone know the answer to that. I feel the importance of the moment and slowly raise my eyes to meet His, they are squinting at me. I'm opened up and laid bare as He searches me through and through. I feel faint. I'm so inadequate. So unworthy. What if He decides I'm not good enough? What if He doesn't want to use me? It's okay, all I want is to be in His court, by the gate, on the floor, anywhere, just as long as I can still touch His garment. Just so long as I don't become a chicken. Jesus speaks without moving His eyes. He quotes my favourite passage from the story of PACLA. It was from a message given to the Assembly by a missionary to Nigeria.

"Africa has a genius for creativity and initiative. Indeed Our God, who made the rainbow in all its varied beauty has planted within this continent a rich variety of colour, form and texture, both in His created order and in His people also. You are unique in His creation and I firmly believe that the contribution Africa has to make to world mission is also unique. It is a contribution which must be entirely, significantly and authentically African."

My Africa. A continent as diverse as it is large. A people as beautiful and vibrant as the myriads of cultures and traditions they represent. A continent of such sweet simplicity, yet unfathomable complexity. It is hard to imagine another continent in which such extremes are played out daily in every arena of life. A continent of such extravagant beauty, yet capable of some of the worst evil ever seen in this century.

Could Africa hold the key to America's renewal? Certainly Africans expressed the joy of the Lord with such passion and zeal that their evangelistic fervor was playing a crucial part in the expansion of the church in Africa. Could this passion possibly be for export? Could it be like Michael (Cassidy) said that in the twenty-first century the fulcrum of world missions will have shifted from the western world to Africa? I pinch myself. Am I African and alive in this era of Christian history?

I am convinced that, yes, Africa does have the answer, but not until the Africans themselves are united. Throughout this book I have made the call to fathers, mothers, young people, old people, and every age group in between. Now it's time to call the Africans. We have a treasure the world needs. Western people in the twilight of materialism are now realizing they have wasted their day dissecting atoms and exploring the galaxies instead of seeking the God who made them. The African church with its expressive Christianity has a responsibility to the wider world, but first it must be strengthened to evangelize Africa and be a church in Africa. We must work together to restore our war-torn continent.

As in America, only the gospel of Jesus Christ can save us now. Only the blood of Jesus can erase the tribalism and racism we each harbour in our hearts and is keeping us at war with one another. Only the blood of Jesus can break through the selfishness of those of us who 'have' and turn it into compassion for those who 'have not.' Only the miracle-working power of that blood can erase the crippling system of bribery that has grabbed our hearts and twisted our minds.

We need to go back to our roots and discover the wonderful ways our grandparents, and the generations before them, worked together to create a safe and healthy environment for their children. They were strong men and women of great love and wonderful traditions and values. They put their emphasis on the community. An individual was nothing without the whole. Today, we have adopted too many negative western values that we need to shed as soon as possible because we are already severely crippled by them. We must rediscover our Lord in order to rediscover each other. We must do that for our children. We have reached the bottom, we have nothing to lose and everything to gain.

I, more than anyone, am painfully aware of the great diversity that exists among us. Some of us were raised Muslim, others Catholic, others Protestant, and still others were raised in traditional African faiths. Then we come from over 800 different ethnic groups and speak over 2,000 dialects. There are almost 600 million of us living on a continent three to four times the size of the continental U.S., and struggling to survive with every geographical terrain known to man.

Some of us have received elementary education, others have gone on to pursue doctoral degrees at Harvard and Oxford. Some sit in some of the highest seats of law, many others have absolutely no rights. Some are doctors, many have never even been to a clinic. Some write books, many cannot read. What we have in common, however, is that we all live in post-colonial Africa.

Africa has entered her fourth decade of independence after three of the most turbulent decades in current history. Whether we want to or not we have to move with the rest of the world in the direction of technological transformation...straddled precariously between the old and the new. We are facing challenges in the 1990s that our fathers and mothers never had to face and therefore have no answers to. Where do we turn for answers to the multitudes of psychological, emotional and physical problems that are the result of the new morality?

How do we stop AIDS from killing off the rest of us that survived the wars? How do we stop the genocide and turn the tide on the huge refugee problem we have? How long will it take for us to stop the fighting and build a future for that specimen of pure wonder--the African child? How do we put a stop to the pain and hardships our mothers experience as widows of senseless wars that continue to ravage our continent from Cape to Cairo? How do we ensure that our men have the ability to provide adequately for their families? When do we save our young men and women from submitting to lives of indignity in the name of survival? Why should our fathers lie buried in the ground, their lives cut off before their time? Why should we live on the richest continent in the world and be so poor, so sick, so hungry?Why?Why? Why?

My brothers and sisters, it is time for an intelligent Christianity. The destiny of Africa in world missions is a present reality to be grasped. We are on the precipice of great change, there has never been a better time to have been born African. Let us not sleep through our day. Now is the time to set the course that will give our people hope of a new life, a life without confusion, hunger, pain and poverty. We must boldly and courageously take on our mission to keep reminding the rest of the world of the arresting power of the Word of God.

The first step we must all take individually is to make a commitment to God, a commitment to be the person God made us to be. This then will become a commitment to fight for an Africa that is all that God intended it to be. We cannot, as much as we'd like to, divorce ourselves from our colonial past, but we can learn to recognize the depth of our African roots and be proud of ourselves as a people. God made us intrinsically African, and the song of praise He longs to hear from our lips is the African song He originally put into our hearts.

We must fight against those who would have us turn God's magnificent African orchestra, with all its different colours and sounds, into one bland sound. It is my sincere belief that if God had thought our culture and traditions were pagan just because we did not wear three-piece suits in the scorching sun of Africa, then He would have created us differently...or given us a different climate.

What breaks my heart the most is to see the rags that were thrown at us still hanging on our children's backs, torn, dirty, ill-fitting. We must return to our Maker in this search to regain our self-respect and dignity, and the dignity of our innocent children, because only at our Father's feet will we find the courage and the freedom to reclaim our minds, our hearts, our bodies. We no longer need to fight for recognition in a world system that is carefully designed to keep us insignificant and enslaved. Christ set us free. We must not be in bondage to other people's standards or systems.

We must STOP placing the blame for our inadequacies outside ourselves so that we may discover the potential within. I have traveled quite a bit, seen a few places, and, yes...seen a lot of faces, but never in the world have I seen the strength of spirit that I see in African faces. The African has the spirit of perseverance that is an inspiration to all. I now call out for us to use that abundant spirit to unite. We must heal the past in order to live the present and dream the future. Only at the Cross will we find the love that will bind us together as a people into one family, one nation under God.

The call is for leaders. Africa is in dire need of leaders with strong moral convictions to serve God in different roles and capacities. There is a great need for young men and women of integrity and character to rise up and fill the shoes of the mighty men and women of God we lost in the eighties. Our problems are so immense that they will take nothing short of our collective spiritual, political and intellectual will and conscience because the world we have inherited is in crisis. Our past political leadership, and much of our present, has left us a legacy of turmoil and confusion.

We are indeed being sent out as sheep in the midst of wolves, we must be shrewd yet innocent as doves. We must engage the mind. Gone are the days of the 'green' African, in are the days of the African standing in the absolute liberty of Christ, controlled by none, yet servant to all. We must assertively bring Jesus into the forefront of the fight for our nation's future. In the book *Heritage of Freedom*, I have read about the truly miraculous events that came about when men and women rose up and united in Christ to change the course of history, turning their countries from destruction to prosperity. Since each generation leaves a legacy for the next to follow, my desire is to see African

Christians rising up and setting a standard of excellence for the upcoming generations to follow. We are the masters of our own fate and must face up to and tackle the issues facing Africa. I would like to see us working together towards the day when not a single African child will die from hunger or improper nutrition.

I look up from the computer just as Jesus takes the journal from His lap and places it on the table beside me. I keep my eyes on it, afraid to look into His eyes. My hands begin to shake. I've reached the frontlines. From here on out I'm carrying **His** cross. I don't want to fail Him. I don't want to give up when the going gets tough, when the sweat begins to pour like drops of blood, when the nails are pounded in and the cross is raised up. I want to be strong to the end. I want to finish the race and go out like a warrior. Most of all, I want Him to know me when I get to Heaven.

Jesus leans over and takes both my hands in His. I feel my body relax and I breath out slowly.

> *"Those tears... they make all the steps I took to Calvary, all the blood I shed worthwhile. (pause) Are you afraid?*

Yes, a little, okay...a lot. I raise my eyes slowly to meet His. The crease on my forehead disappears. "Yes," His eyes tell me, "I'll know you...as the apple of my eye." An immediate smile lines my face from ear to ear. New strength begins to course through me. What was I thinking about? It's not my battle, it's the Lord's, and where there is a vision there is provision. I wait, hoping my heart doesn't burst. Maybe you can tone it down a little, I'm only human after all. Jesus has no intention of doing that. He promised to bless me to overflowing--He's good for His word. This fare is too rich for my soul, I can't take it sitting down.

Jesus takes the journal from the desk and gives it to me. I take it and jump to my feet. Yes! It's my turn. It's time to call the eagles to WAR. He leans back in His chair, His hands behind His head. He grins as He watches me prance about. Let's go, Jesus, open the doors, let's go get them! Oh, if only it was easy to show them the benefits of such a relationship, but their thought processes are too immature. That is the curse of western Christianity, phony to the marrow. They need a blood transfusion as well as a heart transplant. As I gleefully slice them open, a thought hits me and I stop in my tracks. I look over at Jesus and shake my head. Now I know why we had to go through the tears, so that when I got ready to sound the alarm it would be in...love.

> **"Someone's got to tone down that blowtorch of yours. Now prepare for takeoff. I want to see you fly."**

"Blessed Assurance, Jesus Is Mine." My father's favourite song, and now mine. "This is my story, this is my song, praising my Saviour all the day long." I dance around the living room like a crazy woman, my hands flying all over the place, torn between raising them to the Lord in praise and slaying those wicked dragons. If God is for me, who can be against me?

I've asked Jesus for this to become your story, too, so you may know the joy of praising Him all day long. **The joy of the Lord is our strength.** Nothing is impossible with God. Nothing, but we must ask for weapons of victory, not of destruction. Christianity has two lethal weapons, love and the Bible; together they heal everything in sight. Armed with these two, a spiritual man or woman becomes a lethal weapon in Jesus' war against the devil. Without them we are ducks sitting under a sign post that says 'dead meat.' We are salt that has lost its flavour, good only to be trampled underfoot.

So, in the final analysis what is it going to take? We need to learn to love again. Love is tougher than all. Jesus has already determined what it will take to win the war, all He needs are a few strong, quality-minded champions with uncommon commitment and courage. It is only Jesus who can break the chains that have held us all for so long. He has been proven throughout history and eternity. This is not 'religious stuff,' this is the real thing, a relationship between us and our Father in Heaven. Because we have known God, and have loved Him, and have obeyed His commandments, we will never fail. This is the message that young African Christians, with their keen awareness of the supernatural as the basis of life, are announcing to all mankind as they eagerly rush to Jesus.

"While we're on the subject of flying, you might want to start working on passports for Ken and Jordan. Oh, yes, and visas for Uganda... Kenya...South Africa...Europe... Asia...after all, with all there is, why settle for just a piece of sky?"

"And the words of the Lord are flawless, like silver refined in a furnace of clay, purified seven times." Psalm 12:6.

"Lord, you have assigned me my portion and my cup; you have made my lot secure. The boundary lines have fallen for me in pleasant places; surely I have a delightful inheritance." Psalm 16:5 & 6.

"You have made known to me the path of life; you will fill me with joy in your presence, with eternal pleasures at your right hand." Psalm 16:11.

"But He knows the way that I take; when He has tested me, I will come forth as gold." Job 23:10. *"... May Your love and Your truth always protect me."* Psalm 40:11.

"There is no wisdom, no insight, no plan that can succeed against the Lord. The horse is made ready for the day of battle, but victory rests with the Lord." Proverbs 21:30-31.

"He trains my hands for battle; my arms can bend a bow of bronze." Psalm 18:34.

"It is God who arms me with strength and makes my way perfect." Psalm 18:32.

"For He Himself is our peace, who made both groups into one, and broke down the barrier of the dividing wall." Ephesians 2:14.

I thank God that I had twenty-eight years with my father. I wasn't always equal to his trust, but I was always elevated by it. I learned from him that true love always elevates, always seeks to challenge people to be better than what they thought was in them to be. Now I borrow some lines from *Yentl* to thank him for all he was to me.

> *I remember, Papa -*
> *Everything you taught me!*
> *What you gave me, Papa -*
> *Look at what it's brought me!*
> *There are certain things that once*
> *You have*
> *No man can take away -*
> *No wave can wash away -*
> *No wind can blow away -*
> *No tide can turn away -*
> *No fire can burn away -*
> *No time can wear away -*
>
> *And now they're about to be mine!*
>
> *Papa, I can hear you...*
> *Papa, I can see you...*
> *Papa, I can feel you...*
> *Papa, watch me fly!*

Calling all soldiers.... Calling all warriors.... Calling all eagles.... Calling all Life-Bringers....

...LET'S GET DANGEROUS!